fine Cooking
Thanksgiving Cookbook

fine Cooking
Thanksgiving Cookbook

Recipes for **turkey** and **all the trimmings**

From the editors of Fine Cooking *magazine*

The Taunton Press

The Taunton Press
Inspiration for hands-on living®

The Taunton Press, Inc., 63 South Main Street, PO Box 5506, Newtown, CT 06470-5506
email: tp@taunton.com

Editors: Martha Holmberg, Pam Hoenig
Layout: Susan Fazekas
Photographers: All photos by Scott Phillips © The Taunton Press, Inc., except the following:
Ben Fink: p. 66; Alan Richardson: pp. 68, 95, 98, 111, 140; Karl Petzke: p. 86; Sarah Jay © The
Taunton Press, Inc.: pp. 116–118; Martha Holmberg & Steve Hunter © The Taunton Press,
Inc.: pp. 123, 133; Amy Albert © The Taunton Press, Inc.: p. 137; Mark Ferri: pp. 148–149, 156,
170; Steve Hunter © The Taunton Press, Inc.: p. 223

Fine Cooking® is a trademark of The Taunton Press, Inc., registered in the U.S. Patent and
Trademark Office.

Library of Congress Cataloging-in-Publication Data in progress
 ISBN 978-1-60085-827-7 (alk. paper)

Printed in the United States of America
10 9 8 7 6 5 4 3 2 1

It's All Here

You've hit the jackpot. If you've got this book in your hands, you're going to have the best Thanksgiving dinner ever this year. And you'll have fun planning it, too. So tuck yourself into a comfy armchair, grab a notepad, and start grazing. The beautiful photography might lure you in, but you'll stay for the helpful strategies and techniques and, of course, the dozens of thoroughly tested recipes, created by the expert chefs and cooks who write for *Fine Cooking* magazine.

Here's just a taste of what's inside *Fine Cooking Thanksgiving Cookbook*:

- SOLUTIONS TO THANKSGIVING DISASTERS...like the quickest way to thaw a frozen turkey or how to avoid gluey mashed potatoes
- DOZENS OF HELPFUL TECHNIQUES...like how to make a silky pan gravy, how to make a perfect pie crust, or how to brine your turkey
- MAKE-AHEAD STRATEGIES...including shopping and cooking that can be done weeks, days, and hours in advance
- COOKING TIPS THAT GUARANTEE GREAT RESULTS...like how to prevent cracks in your cheesecake, how to keep mashed potatoes warm, and how to make your pie crust more tender
- SIX DIFFERENT WAYS TO COOK YOUR TURKEY...including grilling it over a charcoal fire
- A WHOLE CHAPTER ON LEFTOVERS...and not just for turkey soup; make tostadas, salads, pastas and more with your extra turkey
- LOTS OF RECIPE OPTIONS...versatile stuffings, cranberry sauces, side dishes, salads, soups, and starters that give you plenty of ways to please everyone at your table
- A GREAT EXCUSE TO BAKE...with an amazing selection of dessert recipes from classics like Apple Cider Pie and Pumpkin Pie with a Leafy Rim to delicious alternatives like Triple Chocolate Cheesecake and Espresso Gingerbread Cake

Whatever you decide to cook, and whatever level cook you are, rest assured you're going to get great results if you follow the careful instructions in each recipe and read the helpful tips and sidebars. This kind of valuable information is what makes *Fine Cooking* magazine different from the rest, and it's why you'll want to hold on to this book for many Thanksgivings to come. And don't forget, if you need more help, more recipes, or more menu ideas for Thanksgiving or any time of the year, visit www.finecooking.com or pick up a copy of *Fine Cooking* magazine on the newsstand.

Here's to a moist turkey, silky potatoes, and the perfect pie!

The editors of *Fine Cooking*

Contents

How to survive Thanksgiving (or any other holiday)

Thanksgiving can be such a paradox: Our goal is to create a warm family gathering, full of relaxed conversation around a beautifully laid table of delectable dishes. The reality is sometimes slightly less than ideal—a stressed-out cook, a messy kitchen, and food that's perhaps not always prepared to its best advantage. Our attempts to make the holiday live up to its reputation often mean we try to do too much (and for a new cook, simply roasting a turkey may seem like too much).

But we all know cooks for whom the kitchen at Thanksgiving is like a playground: They turn out a stunning spread with a smile on their faces and not a hair—or a sweet potato—out of place. Their secret to success is a combination of smart choices and good planning. That same confidence and competence will be yours, too, with help from this book. Over the years at *Fine Cooking* we've worked with the best chefs, cookbook writers, and cooking teachers in the country, and they've generously shared their methods and advice. Our test kitchen has rigorously tested the recipes and evaluated the techniques, and the best of all that expertise is gathered into the following chapters.

Be Realistic

We've come to think of Thanksgiving as the meal at which you serve more food than anyone can eat, but does that really make anyone happy? A few perfectly prepared dishes will be much better appreciated than a buffet's worth of recipes that struggled to make it to the table. Think about what your family and guests like most, think about what *you* like to make and what you feel good about, and build your menu around that. You can also purchase a few extras to round out the menu if you have a good prepared food shop near you.

Whether you ask guests to bring dishes is up to you—some cooks appreciate the contributions, others (the control freaks among us) don't like the surprises that sometimes come in the form of the green-bean casserole from Aunt Ginny. We know of one cookbook author who accepted his guests' offers to help and promptly sent them the exact recipes he wanted them each to make!

Take the Time to Plan

Whatever scale of entertaining is on the docket, planning all the steps far in advance is key. Two hours spent with a pen and legal pad a couple of weeks before Thanksgiving will save you a dozen hours and much gnashing of teeth on the day of the feast.

As with any complex operation, breaking the job into discrete tasks lets you understand what you're dealing with and how and when to accomplish each piece. A detailed task list also lets you gauge your progress and feel more in control as time gets short, guests arrive, and the kitchen heats up.

Start with your menu, because everything will flow from that. If you have time, mark all the recipes you'll use so you can get the details straight for planning. But what some people forget is that it's not just the cooking that takes time and energy; there are other elements of a successful event to be considered: shopping, checking fridge and oven space (you don't want to buy a turkey so big it won't fit in your oven), cooking preparation, table and beverage chores, and juggling the timing so that all the dishes come to the table at their optimum temperature.

Shop in Phases, and Always with a List

Even for those who think a trip to the grocery store is fun, shopping can be tiring, so it's best to break it up into manageable bites instead of doing everything in one grand sweep. Make as detailed a shopping list as you can, and be sure to think beyond the kitchen—what drinks will you serve, what extra table supplies do you need, and what kind of decoration do you have planned? Divide the shopping list into "do-ahead" and "last-minute."

Do-ahead shopping:

- Buy your baking supplies, including butter. You can freeze butter and nuts (well wrapped) up to a month ahead.

- Buy other staples such as canned chicken broth, spices, olive oil, charcoal (if you're grilling your turkey), plastic wrap, and storage containers as far ahead as you can think of them.

- Buy your wine and other special beverages ahead, as well as table decorations, candles, and any special linens or napkins.

- Order your turkey ahead of time, if necessary, to be sure you get the size and quality that you want.

Last-Minute Shopping

Shop for your fresh produce or other perishables the day before, plus anything you may have forgotten in the first round of shopping.

Map Out the Fridge Space

It's not just juggling the timing of various dishes that trips cooks up, it's juggling room in the oven and refrigerator. Especially if you're making dinner for a lot of people, the ingredients can take up an amazing amount of space, which is something you don't want to discover as you're standing amidst a sea of grocery bags filled with perishable food.

Before you go to the store, clean out the fridge, transferring non-essentials to a picnic cooler packed with ice packs. Move drinks to a cooler or an ice bucket (or if you live in a cold climate, try the mudroom or back steps). Look around the kitchen to see what you can clear off to give yourself the maximum amount of workspace, as well as plating and serving space, not to mention room for those "incoming" dirty dishes.

Arrange the shelves in your refrigerator so they will accommodate the turkey and whatever other cumbersome dishes you may have. And look for space-saving storage options: Zip-top bags will hold soups, stocks, salad dressings and greens, and raw or cooked vegetables very nicely, and they take up less space than rigid storage containers. Just be sure to label the bags so you're not guessing which is the vinaigrette for the salad and which is the orange glaze for the cake.

Choose Dishes that Suit Your Appliances

Whether you have a single or a double oven, at Thanksgiving it can seem like you never have enough room. As you're deciding on the menu, think about how each dish gets cooked, and how far ahead it can be made. There's nothing more dismaying than realizing that the turkey—which can take up the whole oven—has three more hours to cook and you've got four more dishes that need to roast…each one at a different temperature.

When making your menu, choose dishes whose cooking can be staggered—perhaps a gratin that can be baked early in the day and reheated in the microwave, a pie that can be baked early in the morning, some roasted vegetables that cook on a sheet pan that can be slipped into the oven while the turkey's finishing up, and a couple of more side dishes that come off the stovetop.

Don't Leave All the Cooking for Thanksgiving Day

The actual cooking can be broken into stages also. There's quite a lot that can be done a week or more ahead, when you may feel a little less pressure. There's nothing more satisfying than waking up on Thanksgiving morning knowing that you've got a shaped and ready-to-bake pie crust in your freezer.

Start by making yourself a timetable, working backward from serving time. Make a list of all the dishes that can be partially or fully prepared way ahead of time, then make a detailed timetable for the day of Thanksgiving. Visualize how it will all come together, starting with the moment you mentally ring the dinner bell and working backward.

If, for example, you want to be eating the main course at 7:00 and your green beans take 45 minutes to prepare and cook, set your starting time for them at 6:15. Build some wiggle room into the schedule, in case you underestimate the time it takes to trim those Brussels sprouts. And be sure to allow time for dishes to rest, when appropriate. There are plenty of gratins and baked goods that shouldn't be served piping hot from the oven; read your recipes completely to see what's best.

Think in big blocks of time and try to front-load so that as much as possible is done in advance.

WAY AHEAD: See what can be made and frozen. This usually includes any stocks or soups, and sweet and savory pastry doughs. You can even roll out your pie dough, line the pan, and freeze it.

A FEW DAYS AHEAD: Look for things that do well in an airtight container for a day or so, such as spiced nuts or crostini, or things that can hang in the refrigerator, such as cranberry sauce, marinated olives, fillings, spreads, or dessert sauces.

A DAY AHEAD: Most dishes can wait happily in the fridge for 24 hours. Make dips or dressings, wash and trim vegetables for various dishes, grate cheeses, cut and dry out bread for stuffing, make puddings, cheesecakes, or other desserts that can rest a day before serving.

THE DAY OF: In the morning, bake the pie, chop vegetables and nuts, cook potato or vegetable gratins and casseroles that can be reheated. Later in the day, roast the turkey and finish other side dishes, so that they're finished a half-hour or so before serving time. If you time it right, all that will be left to manage at the last minute is to make the gravy, reheat some side dishes, dress the salad, and light the candles.

Set the Stage for Success

The most successful dinners are the ones that make guests feel festive and appreciated, and a good way to make that happen is by setting a beautiful table. That not only requires attractive tableware, but the time and space to do something with all those plates and platters.

LOOK FOR PLACES TO KEEP DISHES WARM: If you received a warming tray as a wedding present, this is your day to use it. Covering dishes with foil or plastic and then a dishcloth helps conserve heat, too, and if you plan to reheat a dish in the microwave, be sure your serving bowl is microwave safe, or else reheat the food before you put it into the good china.

MAKE THE TABLE LOOK PRETTY: Pulling together the dishes and linens can take a surprising amount of time, especially when you're trying to juggle the action in the kitchen. Almost every savvy entertainer we know gathers all the tableware ahead of time, and many actually set the table completely the night before. You can keep the glasses upside down and the plates stacked to keep them dust-free.

Identify all your serving plates and utensils and even put a sticky note on each one to indicate which dish goes where. This helps you in the heat of battle and also lets a helpful guest handle that chore.

And while you're at it, go ahead and chill the wine and other cold beverages so you don't overlook that step.

A FINAL TIP: Have your garnishes prepared ahead, from chopped parsley or toasted nuts for sprinkling to lush sprays of sage, rosemary, and thyme to tuck around the turkey platter. You can keep them in small zip-top bags, labeled appropriately, in the fridge so they're ready to pop onto your dishes as they head to the table.

KEEP YOUR COOL

Even with the best planning, things can go wrong at Thanksgiving, but as long as you can keep a cool head (and a sense of humor), you can find a solution to any problem. Here are a few of the most common Thanksgiving mishaps, and our smart solutions for them:

It's Thanksgiving morning and the turkey is still frozen.

The fastest safe way to thaw a turkey is to soak it in cold water. Put the bird, still in its wrapper, in your clean sink and cover with cold tap water. Every half-hour, drain the water and refill the sink. The turkey will thaw at a rate of about 30 minutes per pound.

The turkey is ready, but the stuffing isn't hot enough.

For safety, the stuffing should be at least 165°F (test with an instant-read thermometer inserted into the center), so if it needs more cooking, simply take the turkey out of the oven, scoop the stuffing into a baking dish, and return the stuffing to the oven to bake while the turkey rests before carving.

There are a couple of ways to avoid the problem in the first place: be sure the stuffing isn't too cold when you fill the bird and pack the stuffing loosely, so the heat can penetrate. Or avoid the issue altogether and cook the stuffing in its own baking dish, alongside the turkey. You'll get lots of nice crisp topping as a bonus.

The pan drippings are burned.

Turkey juices, both cooked-on and liquid, are the intense flavor base for gravy, but if yours are burned, don't even think about using them. Try this trick, which won't yield a sauce quite as sumptuous as with drippings, but you'll have a respectable gravy:

Pull off a couple of tablespoons' worth of nicely browned bits of skin and meat from the underside of the turkey, chop finely, and, in a clean skillet, sauté them in bacon fat or butter with minced onion and fresh herbs such as parsley, thyme, and sage. When the onion is well browned and soft, sprinkle some flour into the pan and cook the roux until golden; slowly add your broth, and cook, stirring, until the gravy is the thickness you desire.

The best way to protect your drippings is by cooking the turkey in a heavy roasting pan that's just large enough for the turkey and not more—too much empty space leads to a hot pan. If you do have extra space around the bird, or if you must use a thin pan, coarsely chop an onion or two and sprinkle it around the turkey in the pan to act as a heat absorber. If you need to do this, leave the onion out of your homemade broth, if you can, because the pan drippings will be plenty oniony.

The gravy isn't what you'd call silky-smooth.

Lumps are usually caused by undissolved starch. You can eliminate them by straining the gravy through a fine sieve. If, by straining out the flour, the gravy becomes too thin, either simmer until it has a good consistency, or whisk in a little more starch, but carefully: Dissolve 1 teaspoon of cornstarch in a little cool broth or water, then gradually whisk this in a little at a time until the gravy is thickened. Be sure to let it simmer a few more minutes to cook off any raw starch flavor.

The mashed potatoes have a gluey texture.

This is a common problem that's usually due to overmixing, especially when mixing with a hand mixer or (shudder) a food processor. It's always safest to mash with a hand masher, a ricer, or a food mill. The best bet is to start over, but, in many cases, that isn't possible, so try this fix: Spread the potatoes in a fairly thin layer in a shallow baking dish, top with plenty of coarse breadcrumbs and maybe a little grated Parmigiano, dot with butter, and pop in the oven to bake until the crumbs are golden brown and crisp. If you're lucky, the crunchy crumbs will be so yummy that no one will even notice the texture of the potatoes.

The pumpkin pie looks like the Grand Canyon down the middle.

Custard pies tend to crack either because they're overbaked or because the filling recipe called for more starch than was needed to thicken the custard. If you can manage it, remove the pie from the oven as soon as it just begins to set—the filling will continue to thicken as it cools. But if cracks do appear, it's whipped cream to the rescue. Pipe some lightly sweetened whipped cream decoratively onto the surface of the entire pie. Or slice the pie in the kitchen, cutting along the "fault line" if possible, lay each slice on a dessert plate, and top with a generous dollop of fluffy whipped cream.

THE MOST IMPORTANT THING LAST

While you may be spending a lot of energy on this holiday meal, you can feel good about the fact that there are many more delicious meals to come, as long as you've made enough turkey for leftovers. Sure, hot turkey sandwiches are a must for the first day, but for meals beyond that, we've got a whole chapter of dishes that showcase the bird in exciting, appealing ways, from deeply flavored soups to bright salads to robust Mexican- or Moroccan-inspired meals.

And there's one item that you may have forgotten to write on your do-to list, but that is critical: relax and appreciate the experience. It's easy to get caught up in the planning, the cleaning, the cooking (and the fretting), forgetting the real reason that you're hosting the dinner: to be with friends and family, to celebrate with good food and drink, to remind each other of what counts. So do try to build in a little breathing time for yourself as you pull together your stellar feast. Plan for time to enjoy the cooking, time to chat with the guests as they arrive, time to actually sit at the table and eat the food with everyone. And don't forget time to direct everyone else in the clearing and cleaning up!

Appetizers

The notion of serving appetizers at Thanksgiving may seem beyond the organizational capabilities of some cooks—there are so many other dishes to think about—but we've got a range here to suit everyone's schedule. From simple but delicious marinated olives or spiced nuts (which can be made days ahead), to dishes that ask a little more of the cook, such as caramelized onion tarts or a roasted shrimp cocktail, the recipes in this chapter offer what you need to put your own special touch on the big feast.

SPICY
Maple Walnuts

YIELDS 4 CUPS

These nuts continue to toast a bit from the intense heat of the glaze, so don't overbake them. Leave the ginger slices in the nut mixture for a delicious surprise. Pecans and hazelnuts are also great this way. You can store the cooled nuts at room temperature in airtight containers for up to two days or in the freezer in zip-top bags for two weeks.

¼ cup (½ stick) unsalted butter

⅓ cup pure maple syrup

6 quarter-size slices fresh ginger, halved

1 tablespoon water

1 teaspoon ground ginger

1 teaspoon kosher salt

¼ teaspoon Tabasco sauce, or to taste

1 pound (4 cups) walnut halves

IN A CONVENTIONAL OVEN: Heat the oven to 300°F. Combine all the ingredients except the nuts in a small saucepan and slowly simmer over low heat for 2 to 3 minutes. Put the nuts in a large bowl, pour over the glaze, and stir and toss to coat them with the glaze. Line a rimmed baking sheet with foil and spread the nuts in a single layer on it. Bake for 30 to 40 minutes, stirring at 10-minute intervals. When the nuts look light and almost dry as you toss them, they're done. Don't touch them; the caramelized sugar is extremely hot. Slide the foil onto a wire rack and let the nuts cool completely.

IN A MICROWAVE: Put the butter in the largest shallow dish that fits in your microwave. Heat on high for 1 minute to melt the butter. Add the remaining ingredients except the nuts and heat for 3 minutes on high. Stir to combine. Add the nuts, stirring and tossing to coat them with the glaze. Microwave on high for up to 9 minutes, stirring at 2-minute and then 1-minute intervals to redistribute the coating and prevent scorching. When all the liquid has caramelized, they're done. Don't touch them; the caramelized sugar is extremely hot. Carefully slide the nuts onto a foil-lined wire rack to cool. — BARBARA WITT

Herb-Marinated Olives with
FENNEL & ORANGE ZEST

YIELDS 3 CUPS

These olives are most interesting when made with a mix of two or three types of whole, unpitted olives, especially Kalamata, Niçoise, and Picholine. The flavors develop over time, so you can get them out of the way a couple of days ahead. Just be sure to let them come to room temperature before serving for the most succulent texture and best flavor.

3 cups mixed olives, rinsed and drained well

1 cup extra-virgin olive oil

4 sprigs fresh thyme

3 sprigs fresh rosemary

1½ teaspoons fennel seeds

2 strips orange zest

¼ teaspoon crushed red pepper flakes

1 bay leaf

1 clove garlic, slivered

¼ cup fresh lemon juice (1 medium lemon)

Put the olives in a 1-quart jar. In a small saucepan, combine the oil, thyme, rosemary, fennel seeds, orange zest, pepper flakes, bay leaf, and garlic. Heat on very low for 10 minutes. Pour the oil and seasonings over the olives. Add the lemon juice and close the jar. Turn the jar over a few times to distribute the seasonings; let cool to room temperature. Store in the refrigerator for no longer than four days.

Before serving, bring the olives to room temperature and drain off most of the oil. Don't eat the bay leaf.

— MOLLY STEVENS

CHEDDAR-CAYENNE
Coins

YIELDS ABOUT 4 DOZEN 1½-INCH COINS

To have these oven-ready up to a month before Thanksgiving, make the dough, slice it into coins, and arrange them on a parchment-lined baking sheet. Pop the baking sheet into the freezer for a few hours until coins are frozen, and then transfer them to zip-top freezer bags. When you're ready to serve, arrange them on baking sheets and bake. These are fairly spicy, so use the smaller amount of cayenne if you want a milder kick. Pecans or pine nuts would work in place of the walnuts.

6 ounces (1⅓ cups) all-purpose flour

3 ounces (about 1¼ cups) finely grated sharp Cheddar (or half Cheddar and half Parmigiano-Reggiano)

1 teaspoon table salt

⅛ to ¼ teaspoon cayenne

½ cup (1 stick) chilled unsalted butter, cut into ½-inch pieces

1 large egg yolk

2 tablespoons water

⅓ cup medium-finely chopped walnuts

Kosher salt for sprinkling (optional)

Combine the flour, cheese, salt, and cayenne in a food processor; process until just blended. Add the butter and pulse until the dough resembles coarse crumbs. Stir the yolk and water together with a fork and drizzle over the mixture. Pulse until the dough begins to form small, moist crumbs. Add the walnuts and pulse briefly until the crumbs begin to come together.

Pile the moist crumbs on an unfloured work surface. With the heel of your hand, push and gently smear the crumbs away from you until they start to come together in a cohesive dough. Using a bench knife or a metal spatula, lift up one edge of the dough and fold it into the center (the dough will still be rough, so don't expect a neat, smooth fold). Repeat with the opposite edge, like folding a letter. Turn the dough 45 degrees. Give the dough another smearing and shape it into a 14-inch-long log that's 1¼ inches in diameter. Wrap in plastic and refrigerate until firm, about 4 hours, or up to two days. (The dough may also be frozen for up to a month and then thawed for about an hour on the counter or in the refrigerator overnight.)

Heat the oven to 375°F. Line two large baking sheets with parchment. Using a thin, sharp knife, cut the log into scant ¼-inch-thick slices. Arrange the slices about ½ inch apart on the prepared sheets. Bake until medium to deep golden around the edges, 15 to 20 minutes, rotating the sheets as needed for even baking. If you like, sprinkle the crackers with a little kosher salt just as they come out of the oven. Set the baking sheets on wire racks to cool. When the coins are completely cool, store them in an airtight container for up to two days.

—ABIGAIL JOHNSON DODGE

ROSEMARY-PARMESAN
Coins

These simple, do-ahead "nibbles" are a great way to kick off a Thanksgiving dinner. The dough can be refrigerated for up to two days ahead or frozen for a month before using (to really make things easy at the last minute, use the do-ahead tip described in the introduction to Cheddar-Cayenne Coins, at left). The baked coins will keep in an airtight container for two days.

6 ounces (1⅓ cups) all-purpose flour

¾ cup lightly packed finely grated Parmigiano-Reggiano (1 ounce)

1 generous tablespoon finely grated lemon zest (from 1 to 2 lemons)

2½ teaspoons coarsely chopped fresh rosemary

1 teaspoon table salt

¼ teaspoon coarsely ground black pepper

½ cup (1 stick) chilled unsalted butter, cut into ½-inch pieces

1 large egg yolk

2 tablespoons fresh lemon juice

Kosher salt for sprinkling (optional)

Combine the flour, cheese, lemon zest, rosemary, salt, and pepper in a food processor; process until just blended. Add the butter and pulse until the dough resembles coarse crumbs. Stir the egg yolk and lemon juice together with a fork and drizzle over the mixture. Pulse until the dough begins to form small, moist crumbs that just begin to clump together.

Pile the moist crumbs on an unfloured work surface. With the heel of your hand, push and gently smear the crumbs away from you until they start to come together in a cohesive dough. Using a bench knife or a metal spatula, lift up one edge of the dough and fold it into the center (the dough will still be rough, so don't expect a neat, smooth fold). Repeat with the opposite edge, like folding a letter. Turn the dough 45 degrees. Give the dough another smearing and shape it into a 14-inch-long log that's 1¼ inches in diameter. Wrap in plastic and refrigerate until firm, about 4 hours, or up to two days. (The dough may also be frozen for up to a month and then thawed on the counter for about an hour or in the refrigerator overnight.)

Heat the oven to 375°F. Line two large baking sheets with parchment. Using a thin, sharp knife, cut the log into ¼-inch-thick slices. Arrange the slices about ½ inch apart on the prepared sheets. Bake until medium golden around the edges, 15 to 20 minutes, rotating the sheets as needed for even baking. (Don't overbake or you'll lose the lemon and rosemary flavors.) If you like, sprinkle the crackers with a little kosher salt just as they come out of the oven. Set the sheets on wire racks to cool. When the coins are completely cool, store in an airtight container. —ABIGAIL JOHNSON DODGE

GOAT CHEESE, PESTO &
Sun-Dried Tomato Terrine

This savory layered spread is a pretty addition to the holiday buffet. Making it one day ahead allows the flavors to marry and the cook to breathe easier on Thanksgiving day.

10 ounces goat cheese

¼ to ½ cup heavy cream

Kosher salt and freshly ground black pepper

3 tablespoons basil pesto (homemade or store-bought)

5 oil-packed sun-dried tomatoes, drained and finely chopped

¼ cup pine nuts, toasted in a dry skillet over medium-low heat, stirring a few times, until golden, then coarsely chopped

Extra-virgin olive oil for drizzling

Pita chips (page 20) or crackers for serving

Line the inside of a 2-cup sharply sloping bowl (about 4 inches across the top) with plastic wrap; let the ends extend over the sides a few inches. In a medium bowl, mash together the goat cheese and ¼ cup of the cream with a fork, then season with ¼ teaspoon salt and a few grinds of pepper; add more cream if the cheese hasn't softened enough. Spoon about one-third of the cheese into the lined bowl and pack it into an even layer. Spread the pesto almost completely to the sides over the layer of cheese. Top with another third of the cheese, the sun-dried tomatoes, and all but ½ tablespoon of the pine nuts. Top with the remaining cheese. Pack down, fold the plastic over, and refrigerate for at least 30 minutes.

Half an hour before serving, take the bowl out of the refrigerator. Pull on the edges of the plastic to loosen the terrine from the bowl. Invert the terrine onto a plate, drizzle with a little olive oil, and let sit for half an hour to warm up. Sprinkle with the remaining pine nuts, season liberally with pepper, and serve with the pita chips or crackers. —TONY ROSENFELD

Crudités with
CREAMY ROQUEFORT DIP

SERVES 16

A beautiful display of fresh vegetables will start your Thanksgiving meal on a fresh and not-too-rich note. There is a bit of prep work for this recipe—slicing and blanching the vegetables—but all of it can be done ahead of time, including the dip.

4 quarts water

¼ cup kosher salt

1 pound broccoli

1 pound small or medium carrots, preferably with green tops

1 bunch celery (about 1¼ pounds)

1 medium head radicchio

1 medium fennel bulb, fronds trimmed

8 radishes, preferably with green tops

Creamy Roquefort Dip (page 19)

Combine the water and salt in a large pot and bring to a boil over high heat. Meanwhile, trim most of the stem off the broccoli to separate the florets. Using a small, sharp knife, trim the stem of each floret so it's 1½ to 2 inches long. Starting at the top of the stem (just beneath the tiny buds), cut through the stem lengthwise and divide the floret in half—preferably without using the knife to cut through the flowery buds. Repeat the process, dividing each floret into two to four pieces, until the top of each floret is about the size of a quarter. Have ready a bowl of ice water. Boil the florets until they turn bright green, about 1 minute. Drain the florets in a colander, then plunge them into the ice water to stop the cooking and set the broccoli's color. Drain again.

Trim the carrot tops, but leave about 1½ inches of the green tops intact. Peel the carrots and cut them lengthwise into halves, quarters, or sixths, depending on the size.

Remove the tough outer celery ribs; reserve for another use. Trim the tops of the ribs and about 1½ inches from the root end. Starting with the large ribs, cut each lengthwise into long, thin sticks about ¼ inch wide. Trim the large leaves from the celery heart and cut each rib in the same manner, preserving as much of the smaller tender leaves as possible.

Discard the outer leaves of the radicchio. Trim the root end and cut the radicchio in half through the core. Cut each half into ¼-inch-thick wedges—the core should hold each wedge intact. Trim any stalks from the top of the fennel bulb and cut it in the same manner as the radicchio, but don't discard the outer layers unless they're discolored.

Trim the tops of the radishes, leaving about 1 inch of the green tops. (If the leaves are especially nice, leave a few intact for garnish.) Quarter each radish lengthwise.

Store the vegetables by refrigerating them in separate sealed containers or zip-top bags. You can blanch the broccoli up to a day ahead, but the other vegetables will taste and look fresher if you prepare them no earlier than the morning of Thanksgiving.

When ready to serve, arrange the vegetables on a large platter or in a shallow basket. Mist the crudités lightly with water to keep them looking fresh. Serve with the dip on the side. —TASHA DESERIO

CREAMY ROQUEFORT DIP

You can make the dip up to two days ahead. Crème fraîche is sold in the specialty dairy section of some supermarkets.

1 medium clove garlic

Kosher salt and freshly ground black pepper

½ pound Roquefort or other good-quality blue cheese

1 ½ cups crème fraîche or sour cream

½ cup heavy cream

YIELDS 1¼ CUPS

Peel the garlic, then, in a mortar or with the flat side of a chef's knife, mash it into a paste with a pinch of salt. Transfer to a medium bowl and add the Roquefort. Roughly mash the cheese with the back of a spoon. Stir in the crème fraîche or sour cream and several grinds of pepper, and then add the cream until the consistency is slightly thinner than that of sour cream. (It should cling to the vegetables nicely but not be thick and goopy.) Taste and add more salt and pepper if needed. Refrigerate until shortly before serving. (The dip will thicken in the refrigerator but will return to its original consistency as it comes to room temperature.)

Golden Onion & Thyme Dip with
TOASTED PITA CHIPS

YIELDS ABOUT 2¼ CUPS
DIP AND 32 CHIPS

We've all munched our way through a bowl of onion soup-mix dip before—and loved it. Here's your chance to have a grown-up version, still the same creamy, oniony savor, but so much better. Allow about five pita chips per guest. You can make the dip and bake the chips a day ahead; store the dip in the fridge, the chips in an airtight container at room temperature.

FOR THE PITA CHIPS:

2 pita breads (preferably plain and 8 inches wide)

3 tablespoons extra-virgin olive oil

Kosher salt and freshly ground black pepper

FOR THE DIP:

2 tablespoons extra-virgin olive oil

1 large Spanish or 2 large yellow onions (about 1 pound total), finely diced

Kosher salt and freshly ground black pepper

One 8-ounce package cream cheese

6 tablespoons sour cream

1 scant tablespoon fresh thyme leaves, chopped

Pinch cayenne

MAKE THE PITA CHIPS: Heat the oven to 450°F. Slice each pita into 8 even triangular pieces, then tear each piece apart at the seam to get a total of 32 pieces. Toss them in a large bowl with the oil, ¼ teaspoon salt, and some pepper. Spread in a single layer on a large baking sheet. Bake, flipping after 5 minutes, until the chips are crisped and slightly browned, about 7 minutes total.

MAKE THE DIP: Heat the oil in a large skillet over medium-high heat. Add the onion, season with ½ teaspoon salt, and cook, stirring often, until the onion softens completely and starts to brown, about 9 minutes. Transfer to a food processor, add the cream cheese, sour cream, thyme, and cayenne, and pulse until well combined. Season with salt and pepper to taste. Refrigerate until ready to serve. Serve with the pita chips. —TONY ROSENFELD

Crostini with Beef &
HORSERADISH CREAM

A little sprig of feathery frisée is a fresh counterpoint to the topping. Watercress, another green with an agreeably bitter edge, would substitute nicely. The beef can be cooked a few hours ahead and refrigerated. Bring it to room temperature and slice just before serving.

FOR THE CROSTINI:

16 baguette slices, between ¼ and ½ inch thick (from about 1/2 baguette)

2 cloves garlic, halved

2 to 3 tablespoons extra-virgin olive oil

Kosher salt

FOR THE TOPPING:

½ pound beef tenderloin (about a 1½-inch steak)

Kosher salt and freshly ground black pepper

¼ cup crème fraîche or sour cream

2 to 3 teaspoons prepared horseradish

16 pale, inner pieces of frisée (curly endive), washed and dried

MAKE THE CROSTINI: Position an oven rack 6 inches from the broiler and turn the broiler to high. Rub one side of each bread slice with the garlic and set on a baking sheet lined with foil. Brush the garlic side with the oil and season with salt. Broil until the bread is browned, 1 to 2 minutes. Flip and broil the other side for another 1 minute.

MAKE THE TOPPING: Heat a small, heavy skillet over high heat for 1 minute. Season the beef with ¼ teaspoon salt and some pepper. Turn the exhaust fan to high and sear the beef, flipping after 3 minutes, and then cook, flipping every couple of minutes until it's done to your liking, about 10 minutes total for medium rare. Transfer to a cutting board, let rest for 5 minutes, and then slice the beef thinly.

Mix the crème fraîche and horseradish in a small bowl; season with ¼ teaspoon salt and a few grinds of pepper.

To assemble, top the crostini with a slice of beef, a dollop of the crème fraîche, and a small piece of frisée and serve. —TONY ROSENFELD

Stuffed Mushrooms with
PANCETTA, SHALLOTS & SAGE

YIELDS 30
HORS D'OEUVRES

These can be prepared a day in advance and refrigerated—just let them come to room temperature before baking. Also, hold off on drizzling them with olive oil until just before they go into the oven.

35 to 40 cremini mushrooms, 1½ to 2 inches wide (about 1½ pounds)

3 tablespoons unsalted butter; more for the baking dish

1½ ounces pancetta, finely diced (¼ cup)

5 medium shallots, finely diced

2 teaspoons chopped fresh sage

Pinch crushed red pepper flakes

Kosher salt and freshly ground black pepper

⅔ cup coarse fresh breadcrumbs (preferably from a day-old rustic French or Italian loaf)

¼ cup freshly grated Parmigiano-Reggiano

2 to 3 tablespoons extra-virgin olive oil for drizzling

Position a rack in the middle of the oven and heat the oven to 425°F. Trim and discard the very bottom of the mushroom stems. Remove the mushroom stems and finely chop them, along with five of the largest mushroom caps.

Heat a medium sauté pan over medium heat for 1 minute and then add 2 tablespoons of the butter. When it has melted, add the pancetta and cook until it starts to render some of its fat, 1 to 2 minutes. Add the shallots, sage, and red pepper flakes; cook gently until the shallots are tender, about 4 minutes (reduce the heat if they begin to brown). Stir in the chopped

mushroom stems and ½ teaspoon salt. Cook, stirring frequently, until the mixture is tender, about 3 minutes. Add the remaining 1 tablespoon butter. When it has melted, transfer the mushroom mixture to a bowl and stir in the breadcrumbs and Parmigiano. Season with salt and pepper to taste and let cool slightly.

Butter a shallow baking dish large enough to hold the mushrooms in one layer. Arrange the mushrooms in the dish and season the cavities with salt. Stuff each cavity with a rounded teaspoonful of the filling, or as needed. The filling should form a tall mound. (You may have leftover filling; if you have extra mushrooms, keep stuffing until you run out of filling.) Drizzle the mushrooms with the oil and bake until they're tender and the breadcrumbs are golden brown, 20 to 25 minutes. Transfer to a platter and serve warm. —TASHA DESERIO

BACON-WRAPPED
Ginger-Soy Scallops

YIELDS 2 DOZEN HORS D'OEUVRES

Ask for "dry" sea scallops—they haven't been treated with a solution to maintain their shelf life, so they brown better, have a nicer texture and flavor, and tend to taste fresher than treated, or "wet," scallops.

¼ cup soy sauce

1 tablespoon dark brown sugar

1½ teaspoons peeled and minced fresh ginger

6 very large "dry" sea scallops (8 to 10 ounces total)

One 8-ounce can sliced water chestnuts, drained

12 slices bacon, halved crosswise

Set a rack in the upper third of the oven. Line the bottom of a broiler pan with foil, replace the perforated top part of the pan, and put the on the oven rack. Heat the oven to 450°F.

In a medium bowl, combine the soy sauce, brown sugar, and ginger. If the muscle tabs from the sides of the scallops are still attached, peel them off and discard them. Cut each scallop into quarters. Marinate the scallop pieces in the soy mixture for 15 minutes. Reserve the marinade.

To assemble, stack 2 slices of water chestnut in the center of a piece of the bacon. Put a piece of scallop on top of the water chestnuts. Wrap each end of the bacon over the scallop and secure with a toothpick. Repeat with the remaining bacon, water chestnuts, and scallops (you may not use all of the water chestnuts).

Remove the broiler pan from the oven and quickly arrange the bacon-wrapped scallops on it so an exposed side of each scallop faces up. Drizzle with the marinade. Bake, turning the scallops over once after 10 minutes, until the bacon is browned around the edges and the scallops are cooked through, about 15 minutes total. —LAURA WERLIN

GARLIC ROASTED
Shrimp Cocktail

Roasting the shrimp with garlic gives them a punch that's great with the spicy cocktail sauce. At some fish counters and markets, shrimp are available already peeled and deveined.

1½ pounds jumbo shrimp (16-20 count), peeled, with tails left on, and deveined, if necessary

2 cloves garlic, finely chopped (about 1 tablespoon)

2 tablespoons extra-virgin olive oil

½ teaspoon kosher salt

¼ teaspoon cracked black peppercorns

Cocktail Sauce with Red Onion & Jalapeño (see recipe below)

Heat the oven to 450°F. In a large bowl, toss the shrimp with the garlic, oil, salt, and pepper. Spread them on a heavy-duty rimmed baking sheet in a single layer. Roast for 3 minutes, turn the shrimp over with tongs, and continue roasting until they are opaque and firm, another 2 to 4 minutes.

Transfer the shrimp to a shallow dish, cover partially, and refrigerate. When thoroughly chilled (after about 2 hours), serve them with the cocktail sauce. —RORI TROVATO

COCKTAIL SAUCE WITH RED ONION & JALAPEÑO

Pair this sauce with the Garlic Roasted Shrimp (above) or, to simplify matters, make the sauce and serve it with cooked shrimp that you buy at the market. This sauce is best made a day in advance and keeps well for up to a week.

½ cup prepared chili sauce

¼ cup grated red onion (from about ¼ medium onion; use the large holes on a box grater)

½ teaspoon finely chopped fresh jalapeño

3 tablespoons prepared horseradish

1 tablespoon fresh lemon juice; more to taste

⅛ teaspoon kosher salt; more to taste

YIELDS 1¼ CUPS

Combine all the ingredients in a small bowl. Chill, covered, until ready to use. Just before serving, taste and add more lemon juice and salt as needed.

Soups, Salads
& Cranberry Sauce

S imple, elegant soups and refreshing salads set the stage for the traditional courses to come on Thanksgiving, signaling to your guests that this is indeed a remarkable meal. Our selections are designed not to fill you up but to raise the bar of deliciousness for the holiday. The beauty of a soup is that you can prepare it ahead of time and just heat and serve when guests come to the table. Bright, palate-cleansing salads can be served early in the meal or as a refresher between the turkey and fixings and the desserts. And, of course, cranberry sauce knows its place of honor, right next to the tender turkey.

Silky Leek & CELERY ROOT SOUP

Making this soup a day in advance actually gives it a better flavor. Its rich texture makes it perfect to serve in tiny amounts, like a liquid hors d'oeuvre, but it also works as a more traditional first course.

3 tablespoons unsalted butter	One 1½-pound celery root
2 medium leeks (white and light green parts), trimmed, halved lengthwise, cut crosswise into thin half-moon slices, rinsed thoroughly, and drained	¾ cup crème fraîche
	¼ cup heavy cream; more as needed
	Freshly ground black pepper
1 medium yellow onion, thinly sliced	¼ cup thinly sliced fresh chives
Kosher salt	

In a 4-quart (or larger) heavy-based pot, melt the butter over medium-low heat. Add the leeks, onion, and a generous pinch of salt and cook, stirring occasionally, until very soft and lightly golden but not brown, 15 to 20 minutes. Reduce the heat to low if you see signs of browning.

Meanwhile, peel the celery root with a sharp knife (expect to slice quite a bit off the exterior as you trim). Halve the celery root lengthwise and cut each half into 1-inch-thick wedges. Cut each wedge crosswise into ¼-inch-thick slices (you should have about 5 cups). Add the celery root, 1 teaspoon salt, and ½ cup water to the leeks. Cover and cook until the celery root is tender, 10 to 15 minutes. (Check occasionally; if all the water cooks off and the vegetables start to brown, add another ½ cup water.) Add 4½ cups water, bring to a simmer, and continue to cook another 20 minutes. Let cool slightly.

Purée the soup using a stand or immersion blender (work in batches if using a stand blender) to a very smooth, creamy consistency. Let cool completely, then store in the refrigerator at least overnight or for up to two days.

About an hour before serving, put the crème fraîche in a small bowl and stir in enough of the heavy cream to achieve the consistency of yogurt. Leave at room temperature until ready to serve. (If the cream is too cold, it will cool the soup.)

Reheat the soup. (If it's too thick, gradually thin it with as much as 1 cup water.) Taste and add more salt as needed. Ladle into small espresso cups or shot glasses, if serving as an hors d'oeuvre, or into cups for a first course. Top each portion with a small spoonful of the crème fraîche mixture (it should float on top of the soup). Finish each cup with a pinch of black pepper and a sprinkle of chives. —JILL SILVERMAN HOUGH

Butternut Squash Soup with
APPLE & BACON

SERVES 6 TO 7;
YIELDS 6½ TO 7 CUPS

Smoky bacon, herby sage, and sweet apple give this soup layers of flavor. You can cut up the squash and apple a day ahead, along with cooking the bacon. Just save the bacon grease to use for cooking the vegetables, and reheat the crumbled-bacon garnish to crisp it.

8 slices bacon, cut crosswise into ¼-inch-thick strips

One 2½-pound butternut squash, peeled, seeded, and cut into ½-inch dice (about 6 cups)

1 small Granny Smith or other tart-sweet apple, peeled, cored, and cut into ½-inch dice (about 1 cup)

1½ tablespoons finely chopped fresh sage leaves

1 teaspoon kosher salt

½ teaspoon freshly ground black pepper

4 cups homemade or low-salt chicken or vegetable broth

In a 5-quart (or larger) heavy-based pot set over medium heat, cook the bacon, stirring occasionally, until crisp and golden, 8 to 10 minutes. Use a slotted spoon to transfer to a plate lined with paper towels. Increase the heat to medium high, add the squash, and cook until lightly browned, 4 to 6 minutes (resist the urge to stir it too often or it won't brown). Stir in the apple, sage, salt, and pepper and cook for about 4 minutes (you'll see more browning occur on the bottom of the pot than on the vegetables). Add the broth, scraping up any browned bits from the bottom of the pot with a wooden spoon. Bring to a boil, reduce the heat to maintain a simmer, and cook until the squash and apples are very soft, 6 to 8 minutes. Remove from the heat and let cool a little.

Add about half the bacon to the soup and purée, using a stand or immersion blender (work in batches if using a stand blender). Taste and add more salt and pepper if needed. Reheat and garnish each serving with the remaining bacon. —JILL SILVERMAN HOUGH

Parsnip & Parmesan SOUP

SERVES 5 TO 6; YIELDS 5½ TO 6 CUPS

Salty, savory Parmigiano-Reggiano marries well with sweet parsnips, and fresh oregano pulls it all together. You can make this soup ahead and freeze it, but don't add the Parmigiano, soy sauce, or lemon juice until the day you plan to serve it.

¼ cup (½ stick) unsalted butter

1½ pounds parsnips, peeled, trimmed, and cut into ½-inch dice (a scant 4 cups)

6 ounces shallots, cut into ¼-inch dice (about 1¼ cups)

8 cloves garlic, minced

1 tablespoon finely chopped fresh oregano; plus tiny sprigs for garnish (optional)

1½ teaspoons kosher salt; more to taste

½ teaspoon freshly ground black pepper; more to taste

4½ cups homemade or low-salt chicken or vegetable broth

½ cup (1½ ounces) freshly grated Parmigiano-Reggiano

2 teaspoons soy sauce

2 teaspoons fresh lemon juice

Melt the butter in a 5-quart (or larger) heavy-based pot set over medium heat. While it's still foaming, add the parsnips and cook until lightly browned, 7 to 10 minutes (resist the urge to stir too often or they won't brown). Stir in the shallots, garlic, chopped oregano, salt, and pepper and cook, stirring occasionally, until the shallots are very limp and the entire mixture begins to brown, 8 to 10 minutes. Add the broth, using a wooden spoon to scrape up any browned bits from the bottom of the pot. Bring to a boil, reduce the heat to maintain a low simmer, and cook until the parsnips are very soft, 6 to 8 minutes. Remove from the heat and let cool somewhat.

Purée the soup using an immersion or stand blender (work in batches if using a stand blender). Stir in the Parmigiano, soy sauce, and lemon juice. Taste and add more salt and pepper if needed. Reheat the soup and garnish each serving with an oregano sprig, if you like.

—JILL SILVERMAN HOUGH

Soups, Salads & Cranberry Sauce 31

Wild Rice & Mushroom Soup
WITH ALMONDS

SERVES 6 GENEROUSLY;
YIELDS 8½ TO 9 CUPS

If you can't find a ham hock, leave it out—the soup will still taste terrific. You can prepare the soup up to three days ahead (to the point just before you add the cream), or it can be frozen for up to a month. When ready to serve, reheat the soup and add the heavy cream and garnishes.

1 tablespoon olive oil

6 ounces sliced bacon (about 7 slices, applewood-smoked if possible), thinly sliced crosswise

1 pound button mushrooms, stems trimmed, wiped clean, and quartered (about 5 cups)

1 large yellow onion, cut into medium dice (2 cups)

3 medium ribs celery, cut into medium dice (1 cup)

1 large carrot, cut into medium dice (1 cup)

½ cup raw wild rice

6 cups homemade or low-salt chicken broth; more if needed

1 smoked ham hock (optional)

15 sprigs fresh thyme, 10 sprigs fresh flat-leaf parsley, 6 sprigs fresh sage, and 1 bay leaf, tied together with kitchen twine

5 tablespoons unsalted butter

½ cup all-purpose flour

Kosher salt and freshly ground black pepper

1½ cups heavy cream

FOR THE GARNISH:

½ cup (2 ounces) slivered almonds, toasted in a small dry skillet over medium heat until lightly golden and fragrant

¼ cup thinly sliced fresh chives

Heat the oil in a 5-quart (or larger) heavy-based pot over medium-high heat. Add the bacon and cook, stirring occasionally, until the fat is rendered and the bacon crisp, about 5 minutes. Add the mushrooms, stir well to coat in the bacon fat, and then spread out in an even layer and brown on one side without disturbing them, 4 to 6 minutes. Stir in the onion, celery, and carrot; let cook until the onion is soft, about 5 minutes. Add the rice, stirring to coat. Stir in the broth, ham hock (if using), and herb bundle. Bring to a boil and then reduce the heat to maintain a gentle simmer. Cook, uncovered, until the rice is tender but still toothsome, 30 to 40 minutes.

Meanwhile, melt the butter in a small, heavy saucepan over medium-high heat. Add the flour and whisk constantly until the mixture, called a roux, darkens to a caramel color, 2 to 3 minutes. Set aside off the heat.

Once the rice is cooked, discard the herbs. If you've used a ham hock, fish it out and, when it's cool enough to handle, take the meat off and return the shredded meat to the soup. Discard the bone. Return the soup to a boil and thoroughly whisk in the roux a little at a time. This amount of roux should thicken the soup perfectly. You can adjust the amount to your taste if it's too thick or thin; keep in mind that the cream you'll add later will thin the soup. Season to taste with salt and pepper.

When ready to serve, heat the soup and then add the cream. (If you like a lighter soup, you may not want to add all the cream.) Taste for seasoning and adjust if needed, and thin with broth, if you like. Garnish each serving with the almonds and chives. —RIS LACOSTE

Winter Greens with Black Olive Vinaigrette
& WARM MARINATED GOAT CHEESE CROUTONS

SERVES 8

This salad brings together the bittersweet flavors of winter lettuces, the creaminess of goat cheese, crunchy toasts, and savory, salty black olives. The croutons and the vinaigrette can be prepared in advance, so the whole thing is easy to pull together on the big day.

Two 4-ounce logs fresh goat cheese

¼ cup plus 2 teaspoons extra-virgin olive oil

2 teaspoons fresh thyme leaves, coarsely chopped

Freshly ground black pepper

Eight ½-inch-thick slices baguette or thin Italian loaf, cut on the diagonal

1 large clove garlic, cut in half lengthwise

6 lightly packed cups chicory and escarole (or other winter greens of your choice) ripped into bite-size pieces

1 large Belgian endive

Black Olive Vinaigrette (page 35)

Kosher salt

UP TO ONE WEEK AHEAD: Cut each goat cheese log into four equal rounds, using a thin, sharp knife dipped in hot water. Arrange the rounds in one layer in a nonreactive container. Pour ¼ cup of the oil evenly over the cheese. Sprinkle with the thyme and grind on some pepper. Cover and marinate for at least 2 hours or up to one week in the refrigerator. Remove the cheese from the refrigerator 30 minutes before tossing the salad.

UP TO THREE DAYS AHEAD: Heat the oven to 350°F. Rub the sliced bread all over with the cut sides of the garlic clove. Spread the bread slices on a heavy baking sheet and drizzle with the remaining 2 teaspoons oil. Put the sheet in the oven and toast the bread (without turning) until the edges are lightly golden and the bread is crisp, 10 to 12 minutes. Let the toasts cool on a rack. (These can be stored in a plastic bag at room temperature once they're completely cool.)

UP TO 4 HOURS AHEAD: Wash the chicory and escarole and spin dry well. Store covered with a slightly damp towel in the refrigerator until ready to use. If storing for more than an hour, cover the towel with plastic wrap to prevent the towel from drying out. You can prep the greens the day before, but wrap in paper towels and store in plastic bag with all the air pushed out.)

JUST BEFORE SERVING: Trim off the brown root end from the endive and cut the endive crosswise into 1-inch-thick crescents. Use your fingers to separate the leaves. Discard the firm rounds of core. Toss the endive with the chicory and escarole.

Heat the oven to 400°F. Put the croutons on a rimmed baking sheet and lay one round of cheese on each crouton. Use a knife to spread the cheese so it completely covers the bread, then drizzle the marinade over the croutons. Put the baking sheet in the oven for 5 minutes to heat the goat cheese.

While the croutons are warming, set aside about 2½ tablespoons of the vinaigrette and toss the salad with the remaining vinaigrette. Season the salad with salt and pepper to taste.

Dab a bit of the reserved vinaigrette on top of each of the croutons. Serve the salad on individual plates with one crouton alongside. —MARIA HELM SINSKEY

=✕=

BLACK OLIVE VINAIGRETTE

Because of the saltiness of the anchovies and olives, no other salt is necessary in this vinaigrette. The vinaigrette tastes best when prepared at least one day in advance.

3 anchovy fillets, rinsed, patted dry, and finely chopped

2 tablespoons fresh lemon juice

1 tablespoon red-wine vinegar

2 teaspoons minced shallot

1 teaspoon minced garlic

Freshly ground black pepper

½ cup pitted Niçoise or Kalamata olives, finely chopped

2 tablespoons chopped fresh flat-leaf parsley

¼ cup extra-virgin olive oil

YIELDS SCANT 1 CUP

In a small bowl, whisk the anchovies, lemon juice, vinegar, shallot, and garlic; season with pepper. Let sit for 10 minutes, then add the olives and parsley and whisk in the oil. Store, tightly covered, in the refrigerator overnight. Before using, bring to room temperature and whisk again.

Boston Lettuce Wedges with
MIMOSA VINAIGRETTE

This old-fashioned salad is a lovely first course to a traditional Thanksgiving celebration. It's uncompli-cated, so you can prep all your ingredients ahead. Be sure to hard-boil the egg at least a day in advance.

3 small heads Boston lettuce

2 tablespoons fresh lemon juice

1½ tablespoons Dijon mustard

Kosher salt and freshly ground black pepper

¾ cup extra-virgin olive oil

2 tablespoons chopped fresh flat-leaf parsley

1 tablespoon finely chopped shallot

1 large egg, hard-boiled and peeled

Remove any damaged leaves from the lettuce heads and trim their bases. Cut each head through the core into four wedges. Rinse under cold water, shake gently to get rid of excess water, and then set the wedges on a clean dishcloth to drain, cut side down.

In a bowl, whisk the lemon juice and mustard. Add ½ teaspoon salt and a few grinds of pepper, then whisk in the oil in a slow, steady stream. Stir in the parsley and shallot. Separate the egg white from the yolk. Using the back of a spoon, press the white through a fine sieve. Repeat with the yolk. Stir the egg into the dressing and taste for seasoning.

Arrange two lettuce wedges on each of six large salad plates and spoon the dressing over them. Serve immediately. —JENNIFER MCLAGAN

TWO WAYS TO HARD-BOIL AN EGG PERFECTLY EVERY TIME

1. Place the eggs in a saucepan and add enough cold water to cover by about 1 inch. Put the pan over medium-high heat and, as soon as the water reaches a brisk simmer, set your timer for 8 minutes. As the eggs cook, adjust the heat as needed to maintain a brisk simmer.

2. For this second method, start your eggs as you did for the first method, but once the water comes to a brisk simmer, turn off the heat and let the eggs sit, uncovered, in the hot water for at lest 10 minutes and up to 30 minutes—the water cools gradually, preventing the eggs from overcooking. This is a great method when you're multitasking and can't pay as much attention to the eggs.

Escarole with Green Apple,
CELERY ROOT, TOASTED PECANS
& BLUE CHEESE

SERVES 6 TO 8

This vinaigrette tastes best when made ahead, so prepare it up to two days before serving and store it in the refrigerator, tightly covered. Bring it to room temperature and whisk lightly before dressing the salad.

2 tablespoons cider vinegar

1 tablespoon minced shallot

2 teaspoons Dijon mustard

Kosher salt and freshly ground black pepper

5 tablespoons extra-virgin olive oil

¼ pound good-quality blue cheese, crumbled (about 1 cup)

1 medium head escarole

1 medium Granny Smith apple

1 small celery root

½ cup pecan halves, toasted in a small dry skillet over medium heat until fragrant

In a small bowl, whisk the vinegar, shallot, mustard, ¼ teaspoon salt, and a few grinds of pepper. Let stand for 10 minutes, then whisk in the oil. Add 2 tablespoons of the crumbled blue cheese and stir gently.

Trim off the root end of the escarole with a sharp knife. Tear the leaves into bite-size pieces, wash well, and spin dry thoroughly (you should have about 6 lightly packed cups). Store in a large bowl covered with a slightly damp towel in the refrigerator until ready to toss. (You can do this up to 4 hours ahead; if storing for more than an hour, cover the towel-covered bowl with plastic wrap. You can prep the greens the day before, but wrap in paper towels and store in plastic bag with all the air pushed out.)

Up to 1 hour before serving, peel, core, and dice the apple into ¼-inch cubes. Reserve the apple in a medium bowl. Slice the thick skin from the celery root and dice it the same size as the apple. Add it to the apple and toss with 2 tablespoons of the vinaigrette to prevent discoloration. Cover and refrigerate until ready to toss the salad. (Don't soak the apple or celery root in water to prevent browning—you'll ruin their flavor and texture.)

Ten minutes before serving, toss the escarole and apple mixture with the remaining dressing. Break up the pecans into the salad and toss again. Season to taste with salt and pepper. (The blue cheese will add saltiness, so take care not to oversalt.) Crumble the remaining blue cheese over the salad just before serving. —MARIA HELM SINSKEY

Tip

Dissolve a measured amount of salt in the vinegar before whisking in the oil. When salt is suspended in oil, it won't dissolve unless it works its way into a pocket of vinegar. Because acid, whether from fruit or vinegar, accentuates salt, do your final seasoning toward the end of tossing your salad.

—JENNIFER MCLAGAN

Cranberry-Pear
SALSA

The pears, bell peppers, serrano, and honey add complexity and a gentle bite to the traditional cranberry sauce.

One 12-ounce bag fresh cranberries, picked over and rinsed

1½ cups peeled, cored, and coarsely chopped pears (about 2 medium or 1 large pear)

½ cup seeded and diced green bell pepper

¼ cup honey

½ cup granulated sugar

1 fresh serrano chile, cored, seeded, and minced

1 teaspoon finely grated orange zest

2 tablespoons fresh orange juice

1 tablespoon canola oil

Pinch salt

Coarsely chop the cranberries (or pulse in a food processor until coarsely chopped). Combine all the ingredients and toss gently. Taste and adjust the seasonings. This will keep, tightly covered, in the refrigerator.

—ABIGAIL JOHNSON DODGE

Cranberry Sauce with
ORANGE & ROSEMARY

SERVES 6 TO 8; YIELDS
ABOUT 2½ CUPS

Make this bright, zingy sauce a day or two ahead; the flavors will only improve.

One 12-ounce package fresh cranberries, picked over and rinsed

1 cup granulated sugar

½ cup fresh orange juice

2 teaspoons minced fresh rosemary

½ teaspoon finely grated orange zest

Bring the cranberries, sugar, orange juice, and rosemary to a boil in a large saucepan. Reduce the heat to low and simmer for 1 minute. (Some berries will have popped and some will remain whole.) Remove the saucepan from the heat and stir in the zest. Cover and let cool to room temperature, then cover and refrigerate. Return to room temperature before serving. —PAM ANDERSON

Tip

As the cranberry crop reaches peak harvest time in October and November, cranberries become abundant and sale prices abound. Because cranberries freeze well, it makes sense to snap up extra bags and stash them in your freezer. Later on in the spring or summer, when fresh cranberries have disappeared from the markets, you'll get to rediscover them and use them in all sorts of baked goods, and maybe make a cranberry relish, too.

CRANBERRY-CITRUS
Compote

SERVES 10 TO 12; YIELD 5 CUPS

This cranberry sauce gets cooked in the oven, not on the stovetop, so it's hands-off. You can make it up to a week ahead; store it in a zip-top bag to save space in the fridge.

Two 12-ounce packages fresh cranberries, picked over and rinsed

Finely grated zest of 1 lemon

Finely grated zest of 1 orange

2 shallots, finely chopped (about ¼ cup)

2 cups granulated sugar

½ cup fresh orange juice

½ cup thinly sliced scallions (3 large)

UP TO ONE WEEK AHEAD: Heat the oven to 350°F. Combine the cranberries, lemon and orange zests, shallots, and sugar in a large bowl and mix thoroughly. Turn into a 3-quart glass baking dish and drizzle over the orange juice. Bake, stirring occasionally, until the sugar is dissolved and a few berries have popped open, about 30 minutes. Remove from the oven, let cool thoroughly (the pectin in the excess liquid will firm up when cool), cover, and refrigerate.

ON THE DAY OF SERVING: Remove the compote from the refrigerator early in the day to bring it to room temperature. Fold in the sliced scallions and scrape into a serving bowl. — MICHAEL BRISSON

Cranberry-Orange Relish
WITH GINGER

SERVES 8; YIELDS 3 CUPS

This ginger-tinged relish is tart—a perfect complement to the holiday bird. You can make it a day ahead, if you like.

One 12-ounce package fresh cranberries, picked over and rinsed

1 small navel orange, including the peel, cut into 8 wedges

A generous ⅓ cup roughly chopped crystallized ginger

1 tablespoon granulated sugar

¼ teaspoon kosher salt

Combine all the ingredients in a food processor and process until coarsely ground, stopping once or twice to scrape down the sides of the bowl. Transfer to a serving bowl, cover, and refrigerate until ready to serve.

—DIANE MORGAN

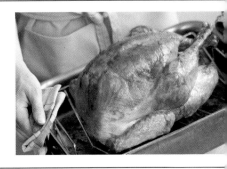

Turkey,
Stuffing & Gravy

When you make a certain dish frequently, you usually get pretty good at it. Most of us have at least a handful of dishes—pasta, pork chops, brownies—that we can whip up without more than a glance at the recipe. But what about a dish you only make once a year? A dish that a roomful of people who've come to visit are very hungry for? A dish that's symbolic of family tradition? A dish that may weigh 24 pounds in its raw state? Yikes. Even an experienced cook can get hung up on pulling off the perfect roast turkey, complete with stuffing and gravy (lump-free, of course).

Taking on the TURKEY

WHICH BIRD TO BUY

When a lot of us were growing up, turkey almost always meant a frozen Butterball, but now there are lots of options for your holiday bird. Frozen turkeys are still readily available, and they're usually the most economical choice. The trick with a frozen bird is to allow enough time for thawing; otherwise, you'll be in big trouble when it comes time to roast. For food-safety reasons, thaw your bird in the refrigerator, not on the counter, and allow two to three days for large turkeys—an overnight stay in the fridge is *not* going to do the trick.

Fresh turkeys are a wonderful choice because they tend to be more moist and juicy. Whether frozen or fresh, we do recommend that you avoid the "self-basting" turkeys, which are injected or marinated in a fat and broth solution to add moisture. We think the cook should be the one to decide what seasonings go into the turkey and there are plenty of good, easy ways to add flavor and moisture to your turkey.

In the fresh category, you have more choices and the labeling can get confusing. Natural means the bird has been minimally processed and no artificial ingredients or colorings have been added; the term does not refer to the way the bird was raised.

Free-range, according to USDA standards, simply means that the birds have access to the outdoors, but what's more important than access is how crowded their conditions are, which is hard to tell from a label. Certified organic tells you a bit more: The birds had access to the outdoors, no antibiotics, and 100% organic feed. And just so you know, no poultry is allowed to be given hormones, organic bird or not.

Kosher turkeys are an interesting alternative to a regular mass-produced turkey. Kosher birds, which are available both fresh and frozen, are grain-fed, free-range, given no antibiotics, and—key to ending up with a moist bird—they've been brined in a salt solution as part of the process required for getting the kosher label.

Tip

Turkey thaws in the fridge at rate of 5 hours per pound. The best way to speed it up is to put it in the sink and cover it with cold water, changing the water every half hour or so. Turkey then thaws at a rate of 30 minutes per pound.

Premium and heritage birds are where the prices really go up, but for the most part, so does the quality and flavor. These are birds that have been raised to give them superior flavor and texture; generally, they're fed a diet that doesn't contain animal by-products, they're free-range, antibiotic free, and allowed to grow more slowly in order to develop fuller flavor. Heritage birds are from traditional breeds thought to have wonderful eating qualities. They're grown on small farms, and many breeds are being saved from extinction by the heritage programs. They have smaller breasts but richer tasting meat.

HOW BIG A BIRD?

The next big question for the cook is "how big?" Any size turkey is likely to be bigger than just about anything you're used to cooking, and Thanksgiving usually means a crowd. Plus leftovers are *de rigueur*. But don't just go for dinosaur size—sometimes biggest isn't best.

First, calculate how much turkey you actually need. Turkey Math, page 48, will help you figure out the size that gives you number of servings plus the amount of leftovers you're looking for.

Next, think about what size bird you can actually accommodate. Once you get over around 16 pounds, you're dealing with a bruiser, and you need to make sure you have a pan that's large and strong enough to hold the turkey and that the bird and your pan will actually fit into your oven (and that you, or someone in your household, can lift the darn thing). Once it's in the oven, you need at least 2 inches of room around all sides of the pan to allow for proper heat circulation (otherwise the times listed in our charts won't be accurate). And remember that a turkey is dome-shaped, so it will need headroom in the oven.

If you have two ovens, a great option is to cook two smaller turkeys, which has the added benefit of more drumsticks, more crisp skin...and two wishbones. Plus, with a small bird, it's easier to get the balance right between fully cooked dark meat and still-moist breast meat.

Tip

Smaller birds fit in the refrigerator better and are easier to handle. If you're hosting a big crowd and have two ovens, consider roasting two smaller birds instead of a large one. (This also gives you a good excuse to try two kinds of stuffing.)

TURKEY MATH

For birds under 16 pounds, figure at least 1 pound of turkey per person. For birds 16 pounds and heavier, figure a bit less since there's more meat in proportion to bone. If you want substantial seconds and leftovers, allow another ½ pound per person

TURKEY WEIGHT (IN POUNDS)	AVERAGE SERVINGS	AMPLE SERVINGS WITH LEFTOVERS
14	14	9
16	16	10
18	20	12
20	22	14
24	26	17

A Turkey Breast is a Clever Option

Another option is to supplement an average-size turkey (which would be around 14 pounds) with one or two turkey breasts, especially if your crowd likes white meat. A boneless turkey breast half weighs about 2 pounds, and it takes beautifully to stuffing with something savory. And on the opposite end of the scale, for a very small crowd—just two or three people—a turkey breast can be a nice way to have tradition without too much fuss. Turkey breasts come either whole on the bone or as a boneless, skinless half.

GET A BIG PAN FOR A BIG TURKEY

So there's your lovely pink turkey, ready for action—what do you put it in? The ideal turkey roasting pan does double-duty, as a secure vessel to hold the bird and all its juices.

Because you only cook turkey once a year, it may seem crazy to invest money in a high-quality roasting pan, but if you do, you'll find that you'll be using use that pan for many other things, such as roasting chickens and meats, roasting vegetables, cooking large batches of lasagna, or using the pan as a water-bath for custards or cheesecake.

CHARACTERISTICS OF A GOOD TURKEY ROASTING PAN INCLUDE:

- Heavy-gauge construction, preferably with a thick aluminum core for good heat distribution and to avoid hot spots or warping at high heat and on the stovetop.

- Strong, stationary handles, as opposed to the kind that are looped hinges, which can be hard to grasp when reaching into a hot oven. The handles shouldn't be so high that they interfere with the oven shelf above.

- Sides between 2 and 3 inches high. Too low and you risk your juices—or even the bird—sloshing over them; too high and the hot, dry air of the oven can't get to the skin to crisp it.

- Rectangular shape with rounded corners, which make it easy for your whisk to chase down those delicious browned bits while making gravy. Oval roasters can look lovely cradling a turkey, but for versatility later in the year, rectangular gives you more room and flexibility.

- Flared lip, in case you want to crimp aluminum foil over the edge (probably not while roasting the turkey, but possibly while cooking crème brûlée for Easter dinner.)

- If your only option is to use a disposable aluminum roasting pan, stack two or three together to give you more stability and to keep the juices from burning.

TO BRINE OR NOT TO BRINE

While we all claim to love turkey, who hasn't had the disappointment of dry white meat? Turkey is fairly lean, the breast meat even more so. The long roasting times needed to get succulent but cooked thigh and leg meat can be brutal for the delicate breast.

As you'll see in the following recipes, there are lots of strategies to deal with this challenge: the position in which you roast the turkey, compound butters slathered under the skin, foil tents. But one method that's becoming more and more popular with savvy cooks is brining. You make a simple salt-water solution—usually flavored with other seasonings such as spices and maple syrup—and soak the bird in it for 12 to 18 hours. Through osmosis, the bird pulls in the liquid, which moistens the meat as it cooks, and adds extra flavor. Note: Do not brine a kosher turkey, as it has already been through this process.

How to Brine a Turkey

MAKE A BASIC BRINE: In a pot that holds at least 6 quarts, combine 1 cup kosher salt, ¼ cup sugar, and 2 quarts cool water. Put the pot over high heat and stir occasionally until the salt and sugar dissolve. Remove from the heat and let cool. Stir in another 2 quarts water and chill in the refrigerator. To jazz up the flavor, you can add herbs and spices, a little flavorful sweetener (like honey or maple syrup), or replace some of the water with another liquid like apple cider or coffee. Just remember that when you add sugar in any form, the turkey will brown faster.

SOAK THE TURKEY IN THE BRINE: Remove the neck, giblets, and tail (if present) from the turkey; reserve them for making turkey broth. Discard the liver. Rinse the turkey well. Double up two turkey-size oven bags and then roll down the edges of the bags a bit to help them stay open. Put the bags in a heavy-duty roasting pan and put the turkey, breast side down, in the inner bag. Pour the brine over the turkey (have someone hold the bags open for you, if possible). Gather the inner bag tightly around the turkey so the brine is forced to cover most of the turkey and secure the bag with a twist tie. Secure the outer bag with another twist tie. Refrigerate the turkey (in the roasting pan, to catch any leaks) for 12 to 18 hours.

RINSE, DRY, AND YOU'RE READY TO ROAST: When it's time to cook the bird, remove it from the brine (be careful, because the cavity may be full of liquid), rinse it under cool water, and dry with paper towels. Now you're ready to follow the rest of your recipe.

NOTE: The brine provides just about all the seasoning you need, so be judicious about adding any further seasonings. Always taste first when making sauces with pan drippings, which tend to be quite salty (if using canned chicken broth as part of the gravy, be sure to use a low-salt one).

STRAIGHT TALK ON STUFFING

Okay, you've picked your turkey and seasoned it to your liking. Now it's time to stuff it, if you like a stuffed bird. Because an improperly stuffed or undercooked turkey can cause illness, please follow these guidelines for safe stuffing.

- STUFF THE BIRD *just* before roasting. You can make the stuffing in advance and refrigerate it for up to two days, but bring it to room temperature before stuffing the turkey because cold stuffing will slow down the cooking. If you like to add egg to your stuffing, don't add it until just before stuffing the turkey.

Tip

Some cooks don't stuff the turkey because they feel it roasts more evenly that way and the stuffing gets a nice crust when it's baked separately. But if you do decide to stuff the turkey and the turkey is done before the stuffing reaches 165°F (the minimum safe temperature), spoon the stuffing into a baking pan large enough to hold it in a shallow layer. Cover with foil and finish baking while the turkey rests.

- PACK THE STUFFING LOOSELY. Stuffing expands as it absorbs juices and, if it's too tightly packed, it won't cook through. A rule of thumb is to leave enough room to fit a whole hand extended into the bird's cavity. Cook any extra stuffing alongside the bird in a casserole dish.

- COOK THE STUFFING IN THE BIRD TO 160° TO 165°F. Check it with an instant-read thermometer inserted all the way into the center of the stuffing. If the bird is done before the stuffing is, take the bird out of the oven but spoon the stuffing into a casserole dish and continue to bake it while the turkey rests before carving.

THE THING ABOUT TRUSSING

The Norman Rockwell image of the Thanksgiving turkey shows the bird's drumsticks neatly tucked against the breast, proudly pointing northward, but in reality, a turkey wants to flop a bit, legs splaying out to the sides, cavity gaping. For many cooks this is not a problem at all and in fact lots of people feel that the bird cooks more evenly when it's not trussed, because the hot air can reach the inner areas of thigh and leg. When a bird is tightly trussed, you increase the density of that hard-to-cook dark meat and it's going to end up taking longer to cook to temperature.

But if you want your bird to look a little better-behaved, loosely tie the ends of the drumsticks together, leaving a bit of space between the legs and body, but preventing them from doing the splits. You should tuck the wing ends under the bird in any case. Or you can go ahead and truss in a more traditional manner, tucking the wings under the bird and running twine from the drumsticks around the body, snugging the legs in tight (see the photos on page 52).

NURTURING THE BIRD DURING ROASTING

Different cooks have different philosophies on how much fussing you should do as the turkey actually roasts; some say close the oven door and forget it, others recommend numerous interventions during the roasting time.

There are a few constants, however. First, even cooking is critical, so rotate the pan a few times during roasting.

Tip

For basting, a wide spoon works even better than a turkey baster, especially at the start when there's little juice.

SIMPLE TRUSSING FOR A NEAT SHAPE

You don't have to truss, but the finished turkey will look better if you do (though it may increase your cooking time).

1. Starting under the legs, draw a length of kitchen twine up and over the legs.

2. Cross the twine between the legs and pull the ends to draw the legs together.

3. Keeping the twine taut to pull the legs in toward the body, run each end over the thighs and wings.

4. Tie securely at the neck.

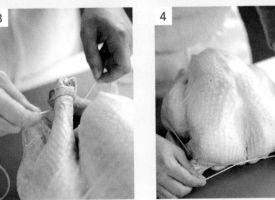

If you're basting the bird, don't baste for the last 20 minutes or so, in order to give the skin time to crisp up. And pay attention to the delicate breast meat, which always cooks quicker than the rest of the bird. If the skin on the breast looks like it's browning too fast, you can cover it with a shield of foil to protect it.

MAKING SURE YOUR TURKEY IS DONE

So the moment of truth has arrived—time to take the turkey out of the oven and present it in all its glory. Or is it? Figuring out when the turkey is done is one of the most difficult and anxiety-producing moments of the Thanksgiving ritual.

Even if you use the same recipe you've always used, every Thanksgiving is a bit different: what temperature was the turkey when it entered the oven, how packed is the stuffing, if it's stuffed at all, how well does the pan conduct heat, how accurate is your oven? But getting well-cooked dark meat and tender moist breast meat is indeed possible, if you use a couple of our tips.

First off, calculate how much time is needed for your size of bird. That's pretty easy—just see our chart on page 54. (There is a debate among cooks about high-heat vs. low-heat roasting, with passionate proponents on each side. You know what? If you pay attention to proper seasoning and cooking time, either method will produce delicious results. Our chart is for roasting at 325°F; for higher temperatures, take off about 30 to 90 minutes total cooking time.)

Second, be sure you have an instant-read thermometer, which can be bought for only a few dollars at any cookware store. This isn't the big dial with the thick spike that your mother may have used, but rather a slender probe that's easy to insert and gives you a temperature reading within seconds. Checking that the dark meat is done (170°F) is key; unfortunately, the breast meat has to stay in the oven as long as the rest of the turkey, so here are a few tricks you can use to keep it from drying out:

- **Rub plain or seasoned butter under the breast skin. The butter will baste and flavor the meat as it cooks.**

- **Start the turkey breast side down. You'll need a rack, but it's worth the investment. As the turkey roasts upside down like this for the first hour or so, it bastes itself. The rack may make a few marks on the skin, but they'll disappear as the turkey finishes.**

- **Give the bird a rest before carving. This allows the juices, which have been forced into the center of the bird from the heat, to redistribute. Don't worry about the turkey cooling off too much; just make a tent out of foil to conserve heat. And you'll need time to make gravy anyway.**

Is It Done Yet?

Wiggling the leg to see if it's loose will give you an indication that the turkey is ready, but unfortunately, by the time the leg is truly loose, the turkey is sadly overcooked. The only reliable test for doneness is to check the internal temperature. Stick an instant-read thermometer in the thickest part of the thigh, without touching the bone. It should read 170°F, and the juices should run clear when you remove the thermometer. The breast meat will always cook more quickly. If the turkey is stuffed, check the stuffing's temperature as well: It must be at least 160°F. If the turkey is done before the stuffing, take the turkey from the oven and scoop the stuffing into a casserole to finish cooking on its own.

APPROXIMATE COOKING TIMES FOR A STUFFED* TURKEY AT 325°F

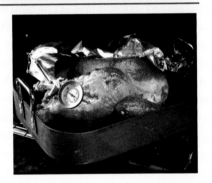

8 TO 12 POUNDS	3 to 4 hours
12 TO 16 POUNDS	4 to 4½ hours
16 TO 20 POUNDS	4½ to 5 hours
20 TO 26 POUNDS	5 to 6 hours

For an unstuffed bird, subtract 20 to 40 minutes from the total cooking time

HOISTING A HOT, HEAVY BIRD

The bird looks beautiful, smells great, but it needs to get from the pan to the platter. Here are a few tips to make this transition as graceful as possible.

Use a rack with handles on the sides so you can lift the turkey away from the pan. To actually lift the bird, whether from a rack or directly from the pan, stick the handle of a thick

wooden spoon in the large cavity between the stuffing (if stuffed) and the underside of the breastbone. Lift the turkey straight up and out of the pan. If your turkey is very heavy, have someone help you move it to the platter by holding the turkey on both sides with paper towels or kitchen towels.

MAKING GRAVY

For some folks, the gravy is the best part of Thanksgiving. Made by thickening the pan drippings and turkey broth with a roux (a mixture of flour and fat), gravy is pure essence of turkey. It's easiest to make it right in the roasting pan, but if your pan isn't flameproof, use a saucepan instead. After you pour off the liquid drippings from the roasting pan, pour some of the broth into the hot roasting pan and scrape with a wooden spoon to capture any cooked-on drippings.

Gravy Math

You'll need about $1/3$ cup gravy per person. For each cup of gravy, use 1 cup of liquid, 1 tablespoon fat, and $1^1/_2$ tablespoons flour. For example, to make 12 servings of gravy, use 4 cups liquid (turkey broth plus defatted pan juices), 4 tablespoons fat, and 6 tablespoons flour.

If you don't have enough broth and pan juices for the amount of gravy you need, add homemade or low-salt canned chicken broth to make up the difference.

=⊰⊱=

QUICK BUT RICH TURKEY GIBLET BROTH

Don't throw away the neck and giblets that come with your turkey. They can be turned into a tasty broth that makes terrific gravy. There's no need to simmer the broth for hours, either. Sweating the meat in a little oil with some onion before adding water jump-starts flavor extraction, so your broth is ready in just about an hour. You can make the broth up to three days ahead. To get even farther ahead, or to make a double batch, buy turkey parts (such as necks, wings, or backs), make the broth, and freeze for up to one month.

Turkey neck, gizzard, tail, and heart (don't include the liver)

2 tablespoons vegetable oil

1 large onion, cut into 2-inch chunks

Kosher salt

4 cups cold water

1 small carrot, peeled and cut into 2-inch pieces

1 rib celery, cut into 2-inch pieces

1 bay leaf

2 large sprigs each fresh thyme and flat-leaf parsley

8 to 10 black peppercorn

YIELDS ABOUT 3½ CUPS

Chop the turkey neck into three to four pieces with a cleaver. Chop the gizzard in half. Heat the oil in a large saucepan over medium-low heat. Add the turkey neck, gizzard, tail, and heart along with the onion and ½ teaspoon salt. Stir to coat with oil, cover, and cook gently for 20 minutes, stirring occasionally; the meat will release lots of juice.

Add the water, carrot, celery, bay leaf, thyme, parsley, and peppercorns. Bring to a boil, cover, and reduce the heat to maintain a gentle simmer. Simmer until the broth is flavorful, 30 to 40 minutes. Strain the broth and use immediately or let cool. Pick the meat from the neck and tail to add to the gravy along with the chopped gizzard and heart, if you like. — JENNIFER ARMENTROUT

WHAT ARE GIBLETS ANYWAY?

Giblets are full of rich flavor and can add great complexity to your turkey broth. The giblet bag usually includes a heart, liver, gizzard (part of the stomach), and neck, but you may find more or less than one of each in your bird. The liver should not be used for broth, because it will make it bitter, but it's delicious sautéed, chopped, and added to stuffing or to a finished gravy.

GRAVY 1, 2, 3

See page 55 for amounts.

Heat the turkey broth. Pour the juices from the roasting pan into a heatproof cup. Let the fat rise to the top and then spoon the fat you need for the gravy back into the roasting pan. Skim off and discard the remaining fat from the juices; add the juices to the broth. Set the roasting pan over two burners on medium heat. Sprinkle the flour into the pan. Stir with a flat whisk or wooden spoon and cook for about 2 minutes.

To keep lumps from forming in the gravy, slowly pour about ½ cup of the broth into the pan while whisking vigorously to disperse the flour evenly into the liquid. The liquid should thicken quickly and turn gluey. As soon as it thickens, add another ½ cup or so of broth while whisking. Repeat until the gravy starts looking more like a smooth sauce than glue.

At this point, it's safe to whisk in the remaining broth and bring the gravy to a simmer. Add a few sprigs of thyme and simmer for about 5 minutes. Strain the gravy through a medium sieve, season with salt and pepper, and serve in a heated gravy boat or other vessel.

CARVING THE TURKEY GRACEFULLY

Carving the turkey can be the undoing of even the coolest cook. That beautiful shape provides a real challenge when it comes time to cut off intact slices of meat and crisp skin. But it's all very logical, once you understand how a turkey is constructed, so take a look at our illustrations, below.

1. Steady your bird with a fork, but try not to stab it or it will lose precious juices. Begin by cutting through the crisp skin that connects the thigh and the breast.

2. Slice down and back to where the thigh attaches to the bird. Keep as much meat as you can with the thigh, leaving little on the back. Bend the thigh away from the breast. Slice through the joint to separate the leg, twisting the knife a little until the leg comes off.

3. Make a horizontal cut just above the wing, straight into the turkey as far as you can go. This cut allows the breast meat to fall from the bird as you slice.

4. Slice the breast meat on the diagonal parallel to the breastbone. Hold the fork against the breastbone as you carve. Lift off each slice, holding it between the knife and fork, and arrange the slices on a serving platter or plates as you carve. Continue carving until you've sliced all the meat from one side.

5. Cut into the joint above the wing to remove it. Or leave it on for now--it helps stabilize the turkey while you carve the other side. Repeat the carving on the other side of the bird if you need to.

6. With the leg skin side up and the knee facing you, cut through the joint that separates the drumstick from the thigh. (The joint is always a bit further into the drumstick than you think.) Separate the two. Cut the thigh meat away in strips parallel to the bone. Arrange the strips of meat on a platter or plates as you carve. Slice the drumstick in the same manner or serve it whole.

HERE ARE A FEW MORE CLEVER CARVING TIPS:

- Since the knife will have little contact with the work surface, you can carve on a platter, which does the best job of retaining the juices, or on a cutting board with a moat around the edge. Sometimes the juices overflow a moat, so lay a towel under the board or put it in a rimmed baking sheet before you begin. If you carve on a platter, you'll still need a cutting board for the legs.

- You need enough space for your bird, the cutting board, and a serving platter or a stack of dinner plates. If the table is cramped, set up a separate carving station; a small, sturdy folding table covered with a tablecloth works well. Or carve in the kitchen and arrange the slices of turkey on the serving platter.

- Use a long, sharp carving knife or a chef's knife. A large fork helps keep the bird in place, but a regular-size fork will do in a pinch.

- Don't carve more than you need for first helpings. It's better to carve again when it's time for seconds because the meat will stay moister and warmer on the turkey than it will on a serving dish.

a mix-and-match feast

Customize your Thanksgiving offerings, using this basic recipe and whichever of the following gravy and stuffing recipes appeal to you most.

YOUR BASIC
Stuffed Roast Turkey

SERVES **10** TO **12**
GENEROUSLY

This is an excellent basic recipe for a roast turkey with all the trimmings. Choose whatever stuffing or gravy combination sounds good from the recipes that follow, or use your family favorites. To stuff the turkey and have a 9x13-inch dish of stuffing to bake separately, you'll need about 18 cups of stuffing. Some of the following recipes make less, so you can either double the recipe, bake a smaller side dish of stuffing, or choose between stuffing the bird and baking stuffing on the side. For more on stuffing, see page 50.

One 12- to 14-pound turkey with giblets

3 tablespoons unsalted butter, melted, or olive oil

2 tablespoons kosher salt

2 tablespoons dried sage

1 tablespoon freshly ground black pepper

1 teaspoon ground nutmeg

18 to 19 cups stuffing of your choice

About 1 cup Quick But Rich Turkey Giblet Broth (page 56) or low-salt chicken broth

Heat the oven to 325°F. Remove the giblets and reserve them for broth. Rinse and dry the turkey. Rub it inside and out with the melted butter or oil, then season with the salt, sage, pepper, and nutmeg. Loosely pack the central cavity and the hollow under the flap of skin at the top of the breast with 6 to 7 cups of stuffing, tucking the flap under the bird. Spoon the remaining stuffing into a buttered or oiled large baking dish, cover, and refrigerate.

Set the stuffed turkey in a large roasting pan, tucking the wings under the bird. (If your roasting pan has a rack, you can use it, but it's not essential.) Set the turkey in the oven to roast.

AFTER 3 HOURS OF ROASTING: Remove the extra stuffing from the fridge and douse it with the giblet broth. Cover the dish with greased aluminum foil and bake with the turkey for 1 hour, uncovering the dish for the last 15 minutes to brown the top.

The turkey is done when an instant-read thermometer inserted into the thickest part of the thigh, away from the bone, registers 170°F and the juices run clear when you remove the thermometer, about 4 hours in all (18 to 20 minutes per pound for a stuffed bird). If the skin browns too much before the turkey is done, cover the bird loosely with foil. If the turkey fails to brown evenly or sufficiently, use a pastry brush to paint the skin with some of the brown juices in the roasting pan.

Remove the turkey from the oven, let it rest in the pan for 5 minutes, and then carefully transfer it to a platter. Tent loosely with foil and let it rest while you make the gravy, using one of the recipes in this chapter or your own. —GREG ATKINSON

CLASSIC
Bread Stuffing

Your stuffing is only as good as your bread, so while your mother may have used a loaf of sliced white bread, you should look for a heartier, artisan-style loaf.

To get a head start on your holidays, cube the bread up to two weeks in advance, put it in freezer bags, press out all the air, and freeze. To really get ahead, make the stuffing entirely and store it in the fridge up to two days ahead, as long as it doesn't contain eggs. For recipes with eggs, just add the eggs to the mixture right before you stuff the bird. Do make sure to let your pre-prepped stuffing come to room temperature before you stuff the bird, however, so that both stuffing and turkey will cook properly.

For a less rich stuffing, omit the last ¼ cup melted butter and add a bit more broth.

½ cup (1 stick) unsalted butter

3 cups chopped onions

2½ cups chopped celery, including leaves

1 clove garlic, finely chopped

1½ tablespoons chopped fresh sage or 1½ teaspoons dried

1½ tablespoons chopped fresh thyme or 1½ teaspoons dried

2 teaspoons celery seeds

Pinch ground nutmeg

Pinch ground cloves

1 teaspoon kosher salt

One 1-pound loaf good-quality white bread, cut into ½-inch cubes (10 to 12 cups), stale or lightly toasted

½ teaspoon freshly ground black pepper

½ cup Quick But Rich Turkey Giblet Broth (page 56), milk, or dry white wine

1 to 2 cups Quick But Rich Turkey Giblet Broth (page 56) or low-salt chicken broth (optional; use if baking the stuffing separately)

In a large skillet over medium heat, melt half the butter. Add the onions, celery, garlic, sage, thyme, celery seeds, nutmeg, cloves, and salt. Cook, covered, until the onions are soft, 5 to 7 minutes. Remove from the heat. In a large bowl, toss the sautéed vegetables with the bread cubes. Season with the pepper. Melt the remaining butter. Pour it over the stuffing, along with the broth, and toss to coat. The stuffing should just hold together when mounded on a spoon.

Loosely stuff the bird. If baking some or all of the stuffing in a separate dish, pour a cup or two of broth over the stuffing to replace the juices the stuffing would have absorbed from the bird. Bake, covered, until heated through, 45 minutes to 1 hour. For a crunchy top, uncover it for the last 15 minutes of baking. — MOLLY STEVENS

THE THREE KEYS TO SAVORY STUFFING

Most stuffings rely on three major components: the aromatic vegetables and seasonings, the bread, and a liquid to keep the stuffing moist.

Bring out the aromatic flavor of vegetables by sweating them in a little fat. You can get creative about what vegetables you include, but onion and celery are the most common and delicious.

The cubed bread should be stale, one or two days old. If you didn't get your bread in time to let it stale, cut it into cubes and lightly toast them in the oven.

Properly moistened stuffing should just hold together. Stuffing that's to be cooked on the side should be a little wetter; stuffing for the inside of the bird will absorb more juices from the turkey as it cooks.

SAUERKRAUT & RYE
Bread Stuffing

Sauerkraut in Thanksgiving stuffing may seem unusual, unless you're from the Mid-Atlantic region, where it's a tradition. And we understand why it is—this stuffing is moist, tangy-sweet, and robust. Fresh sauerkraut is sold in plastic bags in the refrigerated or deli section in most supermarkets. It must be rinsed before using.

½ pound sliced bacon, preferably thick-cut, cut into ½-inch pieces

2 cups chopped onion

1½ cups chopped celery, including leaves

1½ cups chopped carrots

1 tablespoon chopped fresh thyme or 1 teaspoon dried

1 teaspoon caraway seeds, lightly crushed

1 teaspoon celery seeds

2 teaspoons table salt

½ cup dry white wine or beer

2 cups cored and chopped tart apples

8 cups ½-inch rye bread cubes, stale or lightly toasted

1 pound fresh sauerkraut, rinsed and drained

Freshly ground black pepper

In a large skillet, fry the bacon over medium-high heat until crisp. Remove with a slotted spoon and set aside. Pour off all but 4 tablespoons of the bacon grease and set the pan over moderate heat. Add the onion, celery, carrots, thyme, caraway seeds, celery seeds, and salt. Cook, stirring a few times, until the vegetables begin to soften, about 10 minutes. Add the wine and bring to a boil, scraping the pan to loosen and dissolve the browned bits. Add the apples, cover, and cook until they are tender. Combine in a large bowl with the bread cubes and sauerkraut. Season with pepper; toss to combine. Bake in the bird or in a separate dish as directed in the Classic Bread Stuffing recipe on page 62. — MOLLY STEVENS

ITALIAN BREAD & SAUSAGE
Stuffing

Save some time when making this stuffing by cutting up the bread a week or so ahead of time and freezing the cubes in heavy-duty zip-top bags. Be sure to press out all the air from the bags before sealing to prevent freezer burn.

14 cups Italian bread, like ciabatta, cut into ½- to ¾-inch cubes (about 3 loaves), stale or lightly toasted

⅓ cup olive oil

2 pounds bulk sweet or hot Italian sausage (or stuffed sausage, casings removed)

1 turkey liver (optional), finely chopped

2 large yellow onions, cut into ¼-inch dice

5 large ribs celery, cut into ¼-inch dice

8 cloves garlic, finely chopped

1 tablespoon plus 1 teaspoon fresh thyme or 1½ teaspoons dried

1 tablespoon dried sage

1½ teaspoons kosher salt

½ teaspoon freshly ground black pepper

1 cup sweet Marsala wine

1 cup Quick But Rich Turkey Giblet Broth (page 56) or low-salt chicken broth

Pile the bread cubes into a very large bowl. Set a large sauté pan over medium heat and add the olive oil, half of the sausage, and the chopped turkey liver (if using). Cook, breaking up the sausage with a wooden spoon or spatula into ½- to 1-inch bits, until light brown, about 5 minutes. With a slotted spoon, transfer the sausage to the bowl of cubed bread; repeat with the remaining sausage. In the fat left in the pan, sauté the onions, celery, and garlic until the onions are translucent and just beginning to brown, 8 to 10 minutes. Stir in the thyme, sage, salt, and pepper, cook 1 minute, and then add the mixture to the cubed bread.

With the pan off the heat, carefully pour in the Marsala. Keep your face away from the pan as the wine will sputter. (It's unlikely that it will ignite, but if it does, just back off and let it burn for a few seconds until the alcohol has cooked off.) Set the pan over medium heat and bring the liquid to a boil, stirring to scrape up any flavorful bits in the pan. Boil for 2 minutes and then pour this over the bread mixture; stir until well combined. Taste and add salt and pepper if needed.

Stuff the central cavity and the hollow under the flap of skin at the top of the breast, tucking the flap under the bird. Spoon the remaining stuffing into a greased baking dish. When ready to bake, pour over the turkey broth, cover with greased aluminum foil, and bake about 1 hour, uncovering the dish for the last 15 minutes to brown. — GREG ATKINSON

Fennel & Escarole
STUFFING WITH PINE NUTS

Bookmark this recipe to make all winter long. It's delicious on its own as a casserole, topped with a little Parmesan, as a partner for a roast chicken or roast pork loin. You can cut the fennel, cube the bread, and toast the pine nuts a day ahead to make life easier on Thanksgiving day.

¼ cup olive oil

1½ cups chopped onion

4 cups chopped fresh fennel bulb

2 tablespoons finely chopped garlic

1 tablespoon chopped fresh rosemary or 1 teaspoon dried

1 tablespoon chopped fresh thyme or 1 teaspoon dried

1 teaspoon fennel seeds, lightly crushed

1 teaspoon table salt

1 medium head escarole, washed thoroughly and cut into 1-inch pieces (about 6 cups)

½ cup dry white wine

8 cups ½-inch bread cubes, preferably from a chewy sourdough loaf, stale or lightly toasted

½ cup pine nuts, lightly toasted in a dry skillet over medium-low heat, stirring a few times

2 teaspoons grated lemon zest

Freshly ground black pepper

Heat the olive oil in a large skillet over medium-low heat. Add the onion, fennel, garlic, rosemary, thyme, fennel seeds, and salt. Cook, covered, until the onion is soft and translucent, 5 to 7 minutes. Add the escarole, cover, and cook until wilted. Add the wine and let simmer until some of the liquid has evaporated, 2 or 3 minutes.

In a large bowl, combine the vegetables with the bread cubes, pine nuts, and lemon zest. Season with pepper; toss to combine. The stuffing should just hold together when mounded on a spoon. Bake in the bird or in a separate dish as directed in the Classic Bread Stuffing recipe on page 62, adding extra broth to the dish as needed. — MOLLY STEVENS

Dressing WITH APPLES, BACON & CARAMELIZED ONIONS

SERVES 8

Is it stuffing or is it dressing? If it's not baked inside the bird, most people would say it's dressing. Whatever you call it, this recipe is moist and savory-sweet with bits of apple. You can assemble it ahead, but wait until just before baking to add the eggs and chicken broth. A metal baking pan tends to make this dressing cook more quickly.

Butter for the pan

1 loaf (15 to 16 ounces) day-old rustic-style white bread, cut into 1-inch cubes

½ pound sliced bacon, cut into 1-inch pieces

1 large onion, cut into ½-inch dice (about 1½ cups)

1 tablespoon sugar

2 Granny Smith apples, peeled, cored, and cut into ½-inch dice (about 2½ cups)

3 large ribs celery, chopped (about 1½ cups)

⅔ cup chopped fresh flat-leaf parsley

1 tablespoon fresh thyme leaves, lightly chopped

1 tablespoon chopped fresh sage

1 teaspoon kosher salt

Freshly ground black pepper

3 large eggs, lightly beaten

3½ cups Quick But Rich Giblet Broth (page 56) or low-salt chicken broth

Butter a 9x13-inch baking pan. Spread the bread cubes on a baking sheet to dry at room temperature while you prepare the other ingredients.

In a large skillet over medium heat, cook the bacon until crisp, about 15 minutes. With a slotted spoon, transfer it to a plate lined with paper towels. Pour off all but 2 tablespoons of fat from the skillet; reserve the rest. Put the onion in the skillet and sauté over medium-high heat until soft and lightly browned, about 5 minutes. Sprinkle the sugar over the onion and cook, stirring constantly to prevent sticking or burning, until the onion turns deep golden and the edges caramelize, 3 to 5 minutes. Scrape the onion into a large bowl. Return the pan to medium heat and add 2 tablespoons of the reserved bacon fat, the apples, and celery. Sauté until softened, 5 to 7 minutes. Add the parsley, thyme, sage, salt, and a few grinds of pepper; sauté another 1 minute. Scrape into the bowl with the onion.

When you're ready to bake the stuffing, add the bread cubes and bacon to the bowl of sautéed vegetables and toss; add the salt and pepper to taste. Add the eggs and broth; mix well. Transfer to the prepared baking pan. Half an hour before the turkey is done (an instant-read thermometer in the thickest part of the thigh should read 155° to 160°F), put the stuffing in the oven and bake, uncovered, at 350°F until the top is light and crusty, about 1 hour. —DIANE MORGAN

CORNBREAD PECAN *Stuffing*

YIELDS ENOUGH TO FILL A LARGE TURKEY, PLUS LEFTOVERS

The cornbread will reside happily in the freezer for up to one month, as long as it's well wrapped, so make it ahead to save oven time and hassle on Thanksgiving. If you're baking extra stuffing outside the turkey and you like a crust, don't baste during the final 20 minutes.

FOR THE CORNBREAD:

2 cups cornmeal

½ teaspoon table salt

2 teaspoons baking powder

½ teaspoon baking soda

2 cups buttermilk

3 large eggs, beaten

¼ cup (½ stick) unsalted butter

FOR THE STUFFING:

¼ cup (½ stick) unsalted butter; more melted butter for moistening, if desired

5 slices country-style bacon, cut into 1½-inch pieces

1½ cups chopped onion

1½ cups chopped celery, including inner leaves

2 large shallots, finely chopped

2 teaspoons dried thyme

1 tablespoon dried sage

1½ pounds (3 cups) pecans, lightly toasted on a baking sheet in a 350°F oven

Table salt and freshly ground black pepper

½ cup Quick But Rich Turkey Giblet Broth (page 56) or low-salt chicken broth; more to taste

3 large eggs, beaten

MAKE THE CORNBREAD: Heat the oven to 450°F. In a large bowl, combine the cornmeal, salt, baking powder, and baking soda. Add the buttermilk to the eggs and stir into the dry ingredients, mixing just to combine. Put the butter in a 10-inch cast-iron skillet and set it in the oven to let the butter melt. Swirl the melted butter around the pan and add the batter. Bake until the cornbread is golden on top and a toothpick inserted in the center comes out clean, about 20 minutes. Let cool and then tear into coarse chunks in a large bowl.

MAKE THE STUFFING: Melt the butter in a large, heavy skillet, add the bacon, and brown slowly over medium heat until crisp. Remove the meat; leave the fat and caramelized bits. Add the onion, celery, shallot, thyme, and sage; gently cook over medium heat, stirring often, until vegetables are just tender, 10 to 15 minutes. Toss the vegetables, pecans, and bacon with the cornbread. Season to taste with salt and pepper. Stir the broth into the eggs and add to the stuffing, stirring just until it holds together. Add more melted butter if you like. Let the stuffing cool completely before filling the turkey. Bake any extra in a greased baking dish for about 45 minutes, basting occasionally with juices from the turkey or some of the giblet or chicken broth. —SCOTT PEACOCK

Pan Gravy WITH FRESH HERBS

This classic pan gravy, thickened with a beurre manié *(see A Different Way to Thicken Your Gravy at right) and spiked with herbs, goes well with any roast turkey and stuffing combination.*

Pan drippings from roast turkey

About 3 cups Quick But Rich Turkey Giblet Broth (page 56) or low-salt chicken broth

¼ cup (½ stick) unsalted butter, at room temperature

¼ cup all-purpose flour

About ¼ cup finely chopped mixed fresh herbs (chives, chervil, parsley, thyme, marjoram) or 1 tablespoon mixed dried herbs

Table salt and freshly ground black pepper

After removing the turkey from the roasting pan, tilt the pan so the pan juices collect in one corner. Pour all the juices into a large (4-cup) measuring cup and leave undisturbed so the fat rises to the top. Pour off and discard as much of the fat as you can, carefully reserving all the pan juices underneath.

Set the roasting pan over medium-high heat; when it's hot, pour in about 1 cup of the broth and scrape up the browned juices in the pan. Strain this liquid into the cup with the pan drippings. Add the remaining 2 cups broth; you should have about 3½ cups. Pour the mixture into a medium saucepan and bring to a boil.

Meanwhile, in a small bowl, knead the butter and flour together to make a smooth paste (called a *beurre manié*), and then whisk the paste, a few pieces at a time, into the boiling mixture until the gravy reaches a consistency that you like. You might not need to use all of the *beurre manié*. Reduce the heat to low and simmer for 5 minutes to cook off any floury taste. Stir in the herbs and season with salt and pepper to taste. Reduce the heat to low and keep the gravy warm until everything else is on the table. —GREG ATKINSON

A DIFFERENT WAY TO THICKEN YOUR GRAVY

To thicken with a *beurre manié,* knead equal parts soft butter and flour into a smooth paste.

Bring the strained broth and defatted pan juices to a boil and whisk in the *beurre manié* a bit at a time; let boil a minute or so to thicken and cook off the floury taste. Add more *beurre manié* until you reach the desired thickness.

MADEIRA
Gravy

YIELDS ABOUT 4 CUPS

Madeira is a fortified wine that will add a nutty sweetness to this gravy, which makes it taste wonderful with cornbread stuffing.

Pan drippings from roast turkey

2½ to 2¾ cups Quick But Rich Turkey Giblet Broth (page 56) or low-salt chicken broth

1 cup Madeira wine

¼ cup all-purpose flour

Table salt and freshly ground black pepper

After removing the turkey from the roasting pan, tilt the pan so the pan juices collect in one corner. Pour all the drippings into a large (4-cup) measuring cup and leave undisturbed until the fat rises to the top, about 5 minutes.

Pour or spoon off ¼ cup of the risen fat, put it in a large saucepan, and set the pan aside. Spoon off and discard as much of the remaining fat as you can, carefully reserving all the pan juices underneath. Add enough broth to the juices to make 3 cups; set aside.

Set the roasting pan over medium-high heat. When it's hot, carefully pour in the Madeira, scraping up the browned juices in the pan. Keep your face away from the pan as the wine will sputter. (It's unlikely that it will ignite, but if it does, just back off and let it burn for a few seconds until the alcohol has cooked off.) Bring to a boil, simmer for 5 minutes, and then strain this liquid into the measuring cup with the broth mixture; you should have about 4 cups.

Set the saucepan with the turkey fat over medium-high heat and whisk in the flour. When the flour just starts to turn blond, after about 2 minutes, whisk in the broth and Madeira mixture in a slow stream; continue whisking until the mixture is smooth. Simmer gently for 5 minutes and then season to taste with salt and pepper. Reduce the heat to low and keep the gravy warm until everything else is on the table. —GREG ATKINSON

Turkey Gravy SCENTED WITH PORCINI & THYME

YIELDS ABOUT 1 QUART

The woodsy flavor of porcini makes this gravy something special. Start soaking the mushrooms at least 15 minutes before the turkey is done. If you like, you could sauté about half a pound of sliced cremini mushrooms in butter and add them to the gravy at the last minute.

½ ounce (½ cup) dried porcini mushrooms

1 cup very hot water

1 recipe Quick But Rich Turkey Giblet Broth (page 56) or low-salt chicken broth

6 tablespoons all-purpose flour

2 to 3 sprigs fresh thyme

1½ teaspoons fresh lemon juice; more to taste

Kosher salt and freshly ground black pepper

Add the porcini to the hot water and let soak until softened, 10 to 15 minutes. Fish out the porcini and slowly pour the soaking liquid into the turkey broth, leaving any sediment from the mushrooms behind; you should have about 4 cups combined liquid. Chop the porcini finely.

After transferring the roasted turkey to a cutting board, pour the drippings from the roasting pan into a heatproof measuring cup. Let the fat rise to the top and then spoon ¼ cup of the fat back into the roasting pan. Set the roasting pan over two burners on medium heat. Sprinkle the flour into the pan and use a flat whisk or wooden spoon to combine it with the fat. Cook for about 2 minutes.

Slowly pour ½ cup of the broth into the pan while whisking vigorously to disperse the flour. The liquid should thicken quickly and become gluey. As soon as it thickens, whisk in another ½ cup broth. Repeat until the gravy starts to look more like a smooth sauce, then whisk in the remaining broth and bring to a simmer. Add the thyme and simmer for 5 minutes. Strain the gravy through a medium sieve and stir in the chopped porcini and lemon juice. Season to taste with salt, pepper, and more lemon juice, if needed. Keep warm over low heat until ready to serve. —JENNIFER ARMENTROUT

A NIFTY TOOL FOR DEFATTING BROTH

One way to separate the fat from the pan drippings is to let the liquid rest for a few minutes and then spoon off the fat that rises to the top. A neater way is to pour the pan juices, fat and all, into a fat separator, which looks like a measuring cup with a spout. The spout connects to the bottom of the cup, which allows you to pour off the heavier liquid, leaving the fat behind.

our favorite combinations
plus some delicious twists on tradition

*Some matches are made in heaven—here are
three of our favorites, along with two takes on
brined turkey, a solution for a small feast, and
a traditional option that's not turkey.*

DRY-BRINED
Roasted Turkey | SERVES 10

Dry-brining gives the turkey great flavor and a wonderfully crisp skin, and it's less cumbersome than actually soaking the turkey in a brine. To dry-brine the turkey, sprinkle it with salt and refrigerate it overnight (see details in the recipe).

When preparing this menu, here are some small moves that add up to big time savings: While the turkey is roasting, whisk the flour into the heavy cream; store in the fridge. Measure out the Cognac, vermouth, and broth. Pick and lightly chop the thyme leaves.

One 10- to 12-pound turkey	2 medium ribs celery, cut into 1-inch chunks
¼ cup kosher salt	1½ cups water; more as needed
2 medium to large yellow onions, left unpeeled and cut into eighths	Silky Pan Gravy with Cream, Cognac & Thyme (see recipe on page 76)
2 medium carrots, left unpeeled and cut into 1-inch chunks	Herbed Bread Dressing with Bacon, Chestnuts & Prunes (see recipe on page 79)

THE NIGHT BEFORE: Remove the giblets from the turkey, cut off the tail, if attached, and reserve them for making turkey broth. Rinse the turkey thoroughly. Sprinkle the salt all over it, starting on the back side, then the cavity, and finally the breast. Put the turkey on a wire rack set over a rimmed pan or platter and refrigerate, uncovered, overnight.

ONE HOUR BEFORE ROASTING: Remove the turkey from the refrigerator and let stand at room temperature. Fifteen to 20 minutes before roasting, position a rack in the lowest part of the oven and heat the oven to 400°F. Put half of the onions, carrots, and celery in the turkey cavity. Tie the legs together with kitchen twine. Tuck the wings behind the neck and under the turkey. Scatter the remaining onions, carrots, and celery in a large flameproof heavy-duty roasting pan fitted with a large V-rack. Set the turkey, breast side down, on the rack.

Roast for 30 minutes. Pour 1 cup of the water into the roasting pan and roast for another 30 minutes. Remove the turkey from the oven and close the oven door. With a wad of paper towels in each hand, carefully turn the turkey over so that it's breast side up. Add the remaining ½ cup water to the roasting pan. Return the turkey to the oven and continue to roast until an instant-read thermometer inserted into the thickest part of the thigh, away

(continued)

from the bone, registers 170°F and the juices run clear when you remove the thermometer, about another 45 minutes for a turkey in the 10-pound range, or about another 1 hour for a 12-pounder. (Keep a close eye on the vegetables and pan drippings throughout the cooking process. They should be kept dry enough to brown and produce the rich brown drippings to make gravy, but moist enough to keep from burning, so add water as needed throughout.) Transfer the turkey to a carving board or platter, tent with aluminum foil, and let rest for at least 45 minutes and up to 1 hour before carving and serving.

Meanwhile, make the gravy from the drippings. — PAM ANDERSON

SILKY PAN GRAVY WITH CREAM, COGNAC & THYME

Drippings and vegetables from Dry-Brined Roasted Turkey (page 75)

2 tablespoons Cognac

½ cup dry vermouth

2½ cups Quick But Rich Turkey Giblet Broth (page 56) or low-salt chicken broth

2 teaspoons lightly chopped fresh thyme

½ cup heavy cream

¼ cup all-purpose flour

YIELDS ABOUT 3 CUPS

Set the roasting pan with the turkey drippings and vegetables over two burners set on medium high. Add the Cognac, vermouth, and ½ cup of the broth; cook, stirring with a wooden spoon or wooden spatula to loosen the browned bits in the pan, until the liquid comes to a simmer. Strain the contents of the roasting pan through a large sieve into a large saucepan. Add the remaining 2 cups broth and the thyme and bring to a boil; reduce the heat to a simmer and let simmer to blend the flavors, about 5 minutes.

Meanwhile, put the heavy cream in a small bowl and whisk in the flour to make a smooth paste. Gradually whisk the cream mixture into the turkey broth mixture. Bring to a boil over medium-high heat, reduce the heat to low, and gently simmer to thicken the gravy and cook off the raw flour flavor, about 10 minutes. Keep hot over very low heat until ready to serve.

MAKING A LUXURIOUS GRAVY

Heavy cream is the secret to this rich, silky gravy

DEGLAZE: **Pour in the Cognac, vermouth, and some of the broth; stir with a wooden spatula to scrape the browned bits from the bottom of the pan.**

STRAIN **Pour the contents of the roasting pan through a sieve set in a large saucepan. Press gently to extract all the juices; discard the solids.**

ENRICH: **To add extra body, whisk in heavy cream combined with a little flour, and let the gravy simmer to thicken.**

=⚮=

HERBED BREAD DRESSING
WITH BACON, CHESTNUTS & PRUNES

Prunes and chestnuts give this sweet-and-savory dressing an old-fashioned feel, but the generous dose of fresh herbs keeps the flavors up to date. You can prepare everything a day ahead; just don't add the broth and eggs until right before cooking.

One 1-pound loaf dense French baguette or artisan-style Italian bread, cut into ¾-inch cubes (10 to 12 cups)

1 pound thick-sliced bacon, cut into medium dice

2 medium yellow onions, cut into medium dice (about 3 cups)

2 large ribs celery, cut into medium dice (1 cup)

7 to 8 ounces roasted whole jarred chestnuts, crumbled into small pieces

¾ cup coarsely chopped pitted prunes

⅓ cup chopped fresh flat-leaf parsley

2 tablespoons chopped fresh sage

1 tablespoon lightly chopped fresh thyme

½ teaspoon freshly ground black pepper

2 cups homemade or low-salt chicken broth

2 large eggs

SERVES 8 TO 10

Put the bread cubes on a wire rack and let them dry completely overnight.

Adjust an oven rack to a lower-middle position and heat the oven to 375°F. Put the bread cubes in a large bowl. Lightly grease a 9x13-inch baking dish with a little oil or cooking spray.

In a 12-inch skillet over medium heat, cook the bacon until crisp, 15 to 20 minutes, and then transfer it with a slotted spoon to a plate lined with paper towels. Add the onions and celery to the bacon fat in the skillet and cook until softened, 8 to 10 minutes.

Transfer the onions and celery to the bowl of bread cubes. Add the bacon, chestnuts, prunes, parsley, sage, thyme, and pepper. Whisk the broth and eggs together and add them to the dressing mixture; toss to combine. If there's liquid in the bottom of the bowl, let the dressing sit, tossing frequently, until it is absorbed, 3 to 5 minutes.

Spread the mixture evenly in the baking dish, cover with foil, and bake until completely heated through, about 30 minutes. Remove the foil and continue to bake until the dressing is lightly golden brown and crisp on top, about another 20 minutes.

Maple-Bacon Glazed Turkey
WITH WILD RICE & CORNBREAD STUFFING & BOURBON GRAVY

SERVES 10 TO 12;
YIELDS 12 CUPS STUFFING

This recipe brings so many emblematic American flavors together—maple syrup, bourbon, wild rice, bacon, cornmeal, cranberries—it's just what you want to eat on such an American holiday as Thanksgiving. The recipe calls for canned broth, which gets more flavor from being simmered with the turkey giblets. You can also use a double recipe of Quick But Rich Turkey Giblet Broth (page 56). You can make the cornbread two days ahead and the complete stuffing one day ahead. Follow the package directions to cook the wild rice.

One 12- to 13-pound turkey

5 to 7 cups low-salt chicken broth; more if needed

½ cup dried cranberries

1 cup apple or pear cider

1 recipe Cornbread (page 69), cooled and broken into chunks

1 cup wild rice, cooked according to package instructions

4 ripe pears, peeled, cored, and diced

1 cup (2 sticks) unsalted butter, melted

¼ cup chopped fresh flat-leaf parsley

4 scallions, trimmed, white parts chopped

2 tablespoons chopped fresh sage

1 tablespoon finely chopped garlic

1 tablespoon table salt; more to taste

2 teaspoons freshly ground black pepper; more to taste

6 slices good-quality bacon

½ cup pure maple syrup

3 tablespoons all-purpose flour

2 tablespoons bourbon; more to taste

Remove the neck and giblets from the turkey; discard the liver. Simmer the turkey neck, heart, and gizzard in the broth for about 30 minutes; strain. Rinse the turkey inside and out and pat it dry. Combine the dried cranberries and cider in a small saucepan, bring to a simmer, remove from the heat, and let stand for about 5 minutes (you can also use the microwave for this). Drain, reserving the cranberries and cider separately.

Heat the oven to 350°F.

In a large bowl, toss the cornbread, cooked wild rice, half of the pears, the melted butter, parsley, scallions, sage, garlic, and drained cranberries. Season with the salt and pepper. Stir in about 1 cup of the broth, plus half of the reserved cider.

Loosely stuff the front and back cavities of the turkey. Put the remaining stuffing in a buttered baking dish, cover with aluminum foil, and bake alongside the turkey for the last 45 minutes of roasting, adding a little broth if it seems dry.

Put the turkey breast side up on a roasting rack in a heavy roasting pan, tuck the wings under the back of the turkey, and lay the bacon strips over the breast. Add 1 cup of the broth and the remaining reserved cider to the pan, as well as the remaining pears. Roast for about 3 hours, basting frequently and adding more of the broth if the pan gets dry. (If you use a large roasting pan, you'll definitely need to add broth during roasting.)

During the last hour of roasting, baste the turkey with the drippings and brush it with the maple syrup. The turkey is done when an instant-read thermometer inserted in the thickest part of the thigh, away from the bone, registers 170°F and the juices run clear when you remove the thermometer, 3½ to 4 hours total. Transfer the turkey to a platter; tent it with foil to keep warm. To make carving easier, remove the bacon first.

Pour the juices from the roasting pan into a heatproof 1-quart measuring cup, holding back the fruit. Let the juices sit for at least 10 minutes so the fat rises. Spoon 4 tablespoons of the fat back into the roasting pan; discard the remaining fat. Add enough broth to the juices to make 4 cups. Sprinkle the bottom of the pan with the flour and set over low heat. Whisk the flour and fat together to make a roux, scraping up the bits of dark drippings stuck to the pan. Cook for about 5 minutes, stirring constantly; don't worry if the fruit gets a bit smashed—just whisk it along with the roux. Gradually whisk in the pan juices and broth; cook until the mixture thickens, whisking occasionally, about 5 minutes. Add the bourbon and then taste and adjust seasoning with more salt, pepper, or bourbon. Keep warm over very low heat while you carve the turkey. — BETH DOOLEY & LUCIA WATSON

SMOKED PAPRIKA & FENNEL SEED
Roast Turkey with Onion Gravy

SERVES 10 TO 12, OR 6 TO 8 WITH LEFTOVERS

Be sure to use a flameproof roasting pan so it can go directly over the burner when it's time to make the gravy. You can find pimentón, Spanish smoked paprika, in specialty stores or from online vendors.

FOR THE SMOKED PAPRIKA & FENNEL SEED BUTTER:

6 tablespoons (¾ stick) unsalted butter, softened

1 tablespoon fennel seeds, toasted in a small dry skillet over medium heat until very fragrant, then ground

1 tablespoon sweet pimentón

1 tablespoon chopped fresh thyme leaves (save the stems for the turkey cavity)

½ teaspoon kosher salt

¼ teaspoon freshly ground black pepper

FOR THE TURKEY:

¼ cup (½ stick) unsalted butter, melted

1 large onion, thinly sliced

One 11- to 12-pound turkey, trimmed of excess fat

1 recipe Fennel Salt (page 84)

6 cloves garlic, peeled

Zest of 1 lemon, removed in long strips with a vegetable peeler

4 large sprigs thyme, plus the stems from the chopped thyme above

FOR THE ONION GRAVY:

7 tablespoons all-purpose flour

4½ to 5 cups Quick But Rich Turkey Giblet Broth (page 56), hot or low-salt chicken broth

Combine the smoked paprika and fennel seed butter ingredients in a small bowl until well blended. Set aside at room temperature (refrigerate if making ahead).

Position a rack in the lowest part of the oven and heat the oven to 350°F. Brush a large flameproof roasting pan lightly with 1 tablespoon of the melted butter. Make a bed of the onions in the center of the pan.

Trim off the wingtips of the turkey at the first joint and, if already loose, trim the tail from the turkey. Remove the giblets (discard the liver) and neck and set them aside with the wingtips and tail for making the broth. Rinse the turkey and pat it dry with paper towels. Set the turkey on a work surface and loosen the skin over the breasts by sliding your hands under the skin. Rub all of the paprika-fennel butter under the skin, smearing it over the breast. Brush the turkey skin all over with the remaining 3 tablespoons melted butter. Sprinkle 2 tablespoons of the fennel salt all over the skin of the turkey (sprinkle a little inside the cavity, too). Place the garlic cloves, lemon zest, and thyme sprigs inside the cavity. If you like, tuck the legs into the tail flap (or tie them together loosely if there is no flap).

(continued)

Set the turkey, breast side up, on top of the onions in the roasting pan (there's no need for a rack). Roast for 1 hour, and then baste the turkey with the drippings that have collected in the pan and rotate the pan. Continue to roast, basting every 20 minutes, until an instant-read thermometer inserted in the thickest part of both thighs, away from the bone, reads 170°F, another 1½ to 2 hours. (If the turkey is browning too much, tent it with foil.) Set the turkey on a large platter to rest, tented with foil, for about 20 minutes while you make the gravy.

Set the roasting pan with the onions and juices over medium-high heat (it may need to straddle two burners, depending on your stove). With a wooden spoon, stir up any browned bits stuck to the bottom of the pan and continue stirring for a few minutes, allowing the onions to brown a little more. Sprinkle the flour evenly over the onions and juices and stir until the flour is well combined, 1 to 2 minutes. Start adding the hot broth, 1 ladleful at a time, whisking out the lumps before you add more broth. Continue to add broth gradually, whisking each time until smooth, until you've added about 4½ cups of broth. Add any juices that have collected on the platter around the turkey. Lower the heat to medium or medium low and gently simmer the gravy, whisking occasionally, until it's full-flavored and thickened, 8 to 10 minutes. If it seems too thick, add the remaining ½ cup broth. Season with salt and pepper to taste. Keep warm until ready to serve and then transfer to a gravy boat.

Carve the turkey. Pass the gravy boat and the remaining fennel salt at the table.

—TOM DOUGLAS

FENNEL SALT

Use this fragrant salt to "finish" a dish—sprinkle it on meat or fish after it's cooked and sliced so you get a bit of seasoning with every bite. But it's also a great seasoning to sprinkle on a turkey or chicken before roasting.

3 tablespoons kosher or sea salt

1 tablespoon fennel seeds, toasted in a small dry skillet over medium heat until very fragrant, then ground

1 tablespoon freshly ground black pepper

YIELDS ABOUT 5 TABLESPOONS

Combine the salt, fennel, and pepper in a small bowl. Reserve 2 tablespoons of the mixture for sprinkling on the turkey and transfer the rest to a couple of small, shallow dishes for passing at the table.

MAPLE-BRINED,
Wood-Smoked Grilled Turkey

This recipe takes the turkey out of the kitchen to the patio, a fun change from tradition. Grill-roasting the bird adds a savory smokiness and also frees up hours of oven space. The one downside of a grilled turkey is that you probably won't have drippings for gravy (they usually burn in the grill). Allow a total of 4 to 4½ hours to start the fire, cook the turkey, and let it rest. The recipe is written for a charcoal grill; have a full bag of charcoal on hand, as you'll need to add coals as the bird cooks. You can also use a gas grill by adjusting the burners so the turkey isn't over direct heat. If your gas grill just has two zones, be sure to rotate the turkey often so it cooks evenly.

FOR THE BRINE:

2 cups firmly packed brown sugar

1 cup pure maple syrup

¾ cup kosher salt

3 whole heads garlic, cloves separated (but not peeled) and smashed

6 large bay leaves

1½ cups coarsely chopped unpeeled fresh ginger

2 teaspoons crushed red pepper flakes

1½ cups soy sauce

3 quarts water

Handful fresh thyme sprigs

FOR THE TURKEY:

One 12- to 14-pound turkey

Olive oil for brushing

BRINE THE TURKEY: Combine all the brine ingredients in an enamel or stainless-steel pot big enough to hold the brine and the turkey (pot size is less important if you're using oven bags to hold the brined turkey; see page 50). Bring to a simmer, remove from the heat, and let cool completely. Remove the neck and giblets from the turkey, rinse well, and put it in the cold brine; add water if the brine doesn't cover the bird. Refrigerate for 18 to 24 hours.

COOK THE TURKEY: Remove the bird from the brine, rinse it, pat dry with paper towels, and lightly brush it with olive oil. Prepare the grill by lighting about 30 small pieces of hardwood charcoal, preferably in a chimney starter. When the coals are hot and spotted gray, put an aluminum-foil or foil-coated drip that's at least 1 inch deep in the middle of the grill. Arrange half the coals on one side of the pan and half on the other. Wrap ½ cup or so of wood chips in a double layer of foil and set them on the hot coals.

Put the upper rack of the grill in place and center the turkey, breast side up, on the rack over the drip pan. Cover the grill and partially close the air vents. Regulate the vents to keep the wood chips smoking and the coals burning slowly, checking every 25 minutes or so. Add

(continued)

charcoal periodically. Keep the temperature in the grill between 275° and 325°F. Keep the smoke going for 1½ to 2 hours (add more wood chips as needed) and then remove the chips and continue cooking without smoke until the bird is done. The total cooking time for a 12- to 14-pound bird is about 3 to 3½ hours. Test the turkey with an instant-read thermometer in the thickest part of the thigh, away from the bone; it should read 170°F and the juices should run clear when you remove the thermometer. Remove the turkey from the grill and let it rest at least 20 minutes before carving. —JOHN ASH & JEFF MADURA

GRILL-ROASTING YOUR THANKSGIVING TURKEY

This method works best if you brine the turkey first, but you can also enjoy the smoky, savory flavors of grill-roasting with a regular turkey.

Brine the turkey for fabulous flavor and texture. If using a pot, keep the bird weighted down in the brine with a few heavy plates.

Set up the grill for indirect heat. Arrange charcoal on either side of a large foil-coated drip pan; this will allow heat to circulate around the bird. If using a gas grill, set the burners so the heat isn't directly under the turkey.

Keep the smoking chips in a foil pouch or even a small cast-iron pan. This way, you can easily remove them to control how much smoke flavor the turkey picks up.

Brined Roast Turkey with
SAGE BUTTER RUB | SERVES 12 TO 14

Brining guarantees that this turkey will be moist, and the sage butter adds wonderful autumnal flavor. You can make the butter up to two days ahead. The brining itself takes about a day, so mark your calendar so you can plan ahead.

One 14-pound turkey with giblets (removed and reserved)

½ cup (1 stick) unsalted butter, softened

2 tablespoons chopped fresh sage

¼ teaspoon kosher salt; more for seasoning the turkey

¼ teaspoon freshly ground black pepper

¼ teaspoon Bell's poultry seasoning (optional)

Olive oil as needed

One day ahead, brine the turkey, following the directions on page 49. In a medium bowl, stir the butter, sage, salt, pepper and poultry seasoning (if using) until well combined. Refrigerate if making ahead.

Heat the oven to 350°F and position a rack in the lower third of the oven. Remove the turkey from the brine, rinse it very well, and pat it dry with paper towels. Discard the brine and oven bags. With your hands, gently loosen the skin from the turkey breast and legs, being careful not to tear the skin. Use one hand to distribute the sage butter under the skin and use your other hand outside the skin to massage and smooth the butter as evenly as possible over the turkey breast and as much of the legs as you can get to. Tuck the wings behind the turkey to secure the neck skin and loosely tie the legs together. Rub the turkey all over with a light coating of olive oil and sprinkle lightly with salt (to help crisp the skin). Put the turkey, breast side up, on a roasting rack in a heavy-duty flameproof roasting pan. Put the pan in the oven, with the legs pointing to the back of the oven, if possible.

After the turkey has been roasting for 1 hour, begin rotating the roasting pan (for even browning) and basting the turkey with the pan drippings every 30 minutes or so. If there aren't enough drippings to baste with at first, use a little olive oil until there are. The turkey is done when an instant-read thermometer inserted in the thickest part of the thigh, away from the bone, registers 170°F and the juices run clear when you remove the thermometer. Check in both thighs; sometimes one thigh will be done before the other. The total roasting time will be 3 to 3½ hours. Transfer the turkey to a carving board, tent with foil, and let it rest while you make the gravy of your choice. —JENNIFER ARMENTROUT

Dried Apricot & Date Stuffed Turkey Breast WITH MARSALA GLAZE

SERVES 4, OR
2 WITH LEFTOVERS

If you buy a boneless half turkey breast, it will probably be skinless. You may see bone-in, skin-on breasts as well; ask your butcher to bone it for you.

FOR THE STUFFING:

1 tablespoon unsalted butter

⅓ cup finely chopped onion

⅓ cup pitted and coarsely chopped dried dates

¼ cup coarsely chopped dried apricots

3 tablespoons chopped hazelnuts, toasted on a baking sheet at 350°F until lightly browned

2 tablespoons chopped fresh flat-leaf parsley

2 teaspoons chopped fresh sage

Kosher salt and freshly ground black pepper

FOR THE TURKEY BREAST:

1 boneless, skinless or skin-on turkey breast half (1¾ to 2 pounds)

Kosher salt and freshly ground black pepper

2 slices thick-sliced bacon (about 3 ounces)

1½ tablespoons extra-virgin olive oil

1½ cups sweet Marsala wine

MAKE THE STUFFING: Melt the butter in a 10-inch skillet over medium heat. Add the onion and cook, stirring frequently, until soft and lightly browned, about 4 minutes. Set aside to cool. Put the dates and apricots in a food processor and pulse until finely chopped. Add the hazelnuts, parsley, sage, and sautéed onions and pulse a few more times until everything is minced and well combined. Transfer to a small bowl and season to taste with salt and pepper.

PREPARE THE TURKEY BREAST: Heat the oven to 350°F. Put the turkey breast on a cutting board and, holding your knife parallel to the work surface, slice open the turkey breast horizontally, working from the thicker side of the lobe to the thinner side and not cutting all the way through (see the tips on page 93). Open the turkey breast like a book and season generously with salt and pepper.

Spread the stuffing evenly over half of the opened turkey breast, leaving a little border around the outer edges. Fold the other half of the turkey breast over the stuffing, enclosing the stuffing as much as possible. Lay the bacon lengthwise on top of the turkey breast and tie the breast crosswise with kitchen string in four or five places to hold it all together. Season the turkey on both sides with salt and pepper.

(continued)

Heat the oil in a 12-inch ovenproof skillet over medium-high heat. Beginning with the bacon side down, sear the turkey breast on both sides until nicely browned, 3 to 4 minutes per side. Transfer the skillet to the oven (the turkey should be bacon side up) and roast for 20 minutes. Remove the pan from the oven, flip the turkey breast, return to the oven, and roast until an instant-read thermometer inserted into the center of the breast reads 165°F, another 20 to 30 minutes.

Remove the pan from the oven, transfer the turkey to a large plate, and let it rest, loosely covered with foil, for about 10 minutes.

Pour off the fat from the skillet and discard any lumps of stuffing that may have fallen

out of the turkey and burned. Put the skillet over medium-high heat, pour in the Marsala, and bring it to a boil, stirring with a wooden spatula to scrape up any browned bits on the bottom of the pan. Add any juices that have collected around the turkey while resting on the plate. Continue boiling until the Marsala is reduced to ¼ cup, 5 to 7 minutes. Season with salt and pepper to taste.

Remove the strings from the turkey. Slice the turkey crosswise into ½-inch-thick slices and arrange the slices on a serving platter. Pour the Marsala glaze into a small bowl and pass with the turkey.

— TOM DOUGLAS

HOW TO BUTTERFLY AND STUFF
A BONELESS TURKEY BREAST

A boneless turkey breast is a perfect solution when serving only a couple of people, but the meat can be dry. Tying a couple of strips of bacon onto it adds much needed fat.

Slice open the turkey breast horizontally, working from the thicker side of the lobe to the thinner.

Open the breast and spread the stuffing over half of it, leaving a border around the outer edge.

Lay two slices of bacon lengthwise on top and tie the breast crosswise in several places.

ROAST
Duck or Goose
FOR THE YIELD, SEE BELOW

A duck or goose makes an exciting change from—or addition to—a turkey on the Thanksgiving table, especially for fans of dark meat. But ducks and geese are different from turkey in two important ways: They have a smaller meat-to-bone ratio, so you need to allow more weight per person than with turkey. And these birds are much fattier. To manage the fat, you separate the skin from the meat before cooking, which allows it to render more easily, and you pour off the accumulated fat in the pan during cooking. The succulent, savory meat is ample reward for the extra effort. Ducks weigh 4½ to 6 pounds; allow at least 2 pounds per person. Geese weigh 8 to 10 pounds; allow at least 2 pounds per person.

1 free-range, naturally fed duck or goose

Stuffing of your choice (optional)

2 tablespoons olive oil

2 tablespoons kosher salt mixed with a few grinds of black pepper

1 cup water

Heat the oven to 375°F. Trim any excess fat, rinse the bird inside and out, and pat it dry. Slip your fingers or a rubber spatula between the fat and the meat to separate them, and prick the skin all over with a sharp-tined fork, taking care not to prick the meat. If possible, turn on a fan to let the bird air-dry while it comes to room temperature.

If roasting with stuffing, stuff the bird three-quarters full. Rub the outside with the olive oil, then massage the bird thoroughly with the salt and pepper mixture. Tie the legs together loosely. Put the bird in a roasting pan (preferably fitted with a rack). Pour the water in the pan. Position the pan so that the bird's legs point toward the back of the oven. Roast for 45 minutes. Remove the pan from the oven and pour the fat and water into a heatproof container. Skim off the fat to use for basting.

Return the bird to the oven and increase the temperature to 400°F. Continue to cook for about another 1¼ hours for a duck, another 2 hours for a goose. During this time, pour the grease off once or twice more.

For the last hour of roasting, turn the pan so that the legs face the front of the oven. Refrain from basting for the last half hour of cooking time. The bird is done when an instant-read thermometer inserted into the inner thigh below the leg joint, away from the bone, reads 175° to 180°F; the juices should run clear when the thermometer is removed. A thermometer inserted in the stuffing's center should read at least 160°F. Transfer the bird to a platter and let it rest for 15 minutes before carving. —LARRY FORGIONE

Vegetables

Here's where the creative cook can really show off. While turkey and mashed potatoes are mandatory, the choice of side dishes is wide open, and we provide all the inspiration you'll need to lay a sumptuous spread. From greens to beans to roots and more, our vegetable side dishes are bright-tasting, beautiful, and mostly do-ahead, so don't hesitate to try more than one or two.

Green Beans
WITH BROWN BUTTER & PECANS

You can boil the green beans ahead of time, but you'll need to rewarm them a bit longer in the brown butter, covered, over low heat.

2 pounds green beans, trimmed

½ cup (1 stick) unsalted butter, cut into pieces

¼ cup finely chopped shallots

½ cup chopped toasted pecans

2 tablespoons fresh lemon juice; more to taste

Kosher salt and freshly ground black pepper

Bring a large pot of salted water to a boil. Add the green beans; cook until tender, about 5 minutes. Drain and then plunge them into ice water to stop the cooking. Drain and set aside.

In a large skillet over medium-high heat, melt the butter. Add the shallots and pecans; cook, stirring, until the butter turns light brown and begins to smell nutty; be careful not to burn it. Add the beans, toss to coat, and cook until warmed through, about 3 minutes. Add the lemon juice and season with salt and pepper. —ROBERT CARTER

Garlic-Roasted Green Beans
& SHALLOTS WITH HAZELNUTS

SERVES 8

Chopped hazelnuts are a fine flavor match for green beans—and a refreshing departure from the more-expected almonds. The beans will hold at room temperature for several minutes before serving; cover with foil to keep warm.

- 10 to 12 medium shallots, sliced lengthwise ¼ inch thick
- 2 pounds green beans, trimmed
- 10 medium cloves garlic, coarsely chopped
- 6 tablespoons extra-virgin olive oil

- 2 teaspoons kosher salt
- 1 teaspoon freshly ground black pepper
- ½ cup finely chopped fresh flat-leaf parsley
- ½ cup coarsely chopped toasted hazelnuts
- 2 teaspoons finely grated lemon zest

Position racks in the top and bottom thirds of the oven and heat the oven to 450°F.

Put the shallots, green beans, and garlic in a large bowl; toss with the oil. Sprinkle the salt and pepper over the vegetables and toss again. Transfer to two large baking dishes (about 10x15 inches) and roast until tender and very lightly browned, stirring once, 18 to 20 minutes.

Meanwhile, combine the parsley, hazelnuts, and lemon zest in a small bowl. Sprinkle this over the roasted vegetables when they come out of the oven and toss to coat. Serve warm. —JULIANNA GRIMES

Long-Cooked Green Beans
WITH OREGANO

SERVES 6 TO 8

These green beans don't have your typical "crisp-tender" texture, but rather a tender and slightly chewy bite with deeply concentrated flavor. They taste best when they've had a few minutes to rest after cooking—and they're even great at room temperature—so you won't need to rush to the table.

¼ cup extra-virgin olive oil

6 cloves garlic, chopped coarsely

Leaves from 6 large sprigs fresh oregano (scant ¼ cup)

1¾ pounds green beans (preferably mature), trimmed

2 teaspoons kosher salt

Freshly ground black pepper

3 tablespoons fresh lemon juice

½ cup water

Heat the olive oil in a large, heavy-based pot (like an 8-quart Dutch oven) over medium heat. Add the garlic and oregano and cook, stirring, until fragrant and the garlic is softened but not browned, about 2 minutes. Put the beans in the pot, add the salt, and grind a little pepper over all. Add the lemon juice and water and bring to a boil. Immediately reduce the heat to a simmer, cover, and cook for 20 minutes.

Remove the lid and simmer the beans gently over medium-high heat until nearly all the liquid in the pot has evaporated, about 30 minutes. During this time, occasionally turn the beans over with tongs to mix them and coat them with the reducing juices. Let cool briefly before serving. —PAUL BERTOLLI

Sautéed Swiss Chard
WITH SLIVERED ALMONDS & BROWNED BUTTER

SERVES 6

Swiss chard is a lot like spinach but slightly sturdier, so it takes a few minutes longer to cook but holds up well if it needs to wait a bit to be served. To get ahead, wash, trim, and cut the chard up to a day ahead and keep it tightly sealed in the refrigerator.

2 pounds Swiss chard (from about 2 bunches)

2 tablespoons unsalted butter

⅓ cup slivered almonds

1 teaspoon fresh lemon juice

2 tablespoons extra-virgin olive oil

2 tablespoons finely chopped shallot

Kosher salt

Pinch crushed red pepper flakes

Fill a sink with cold water and wash the Swiss chard to remove any grit. Transfer to paper towels and let dry for a couple of minutes (it's fine if a little water clings to the leaves).

Remove the thick part of each stem by cutting a V-shaped notch partway into the leaf. Split each leaf in half lengthwise by slicing down the center rib. Stack the halved leaves (in batches if necessary) and cut them in half crosswise to get 4- to 6-inch pieces.

In a small sauté pan or saucepan, melt the butter over medium heat. Add the almonds, reduce the heat to medium low, and cook, stirring often, until the nuts are golden and the milk solids in the butter turn a nutty brown. Remove from the heat and stir in the lemon juice. Keep warm.

Heat the oil in a large skillet over medium-high heat for 1 minute. Working in batches, pile the Swiss chard into the pan, turning and tossing gently until the leaves begin to wilt and turn glossy. Add a new batch of leaves as the previous batch wilts and makes room for more.

When all the chard is wilted, sprinkle in the shallot and a little salt and toss well. Reduce the heat to medium low, cover, and cook for 4 minutes. Remove the lid, raise the heat to high, add the red pepper flakes, and continue to cook for 2 minutes so that much of the liquid evaporates; the leaves should be tender but not overly soft. Sprinkle the almonds and melted butter over the finished chard and serve immediately. —ARLENE JACOBS

FIRM, GLOSSY SWISS CHARD

Until recently, red- or white-stemmed chard was mostly what you found in markets, but the beautiful Bright Lights variety is now easier to come by. The colors don't make a huge flavor difference, but do know that those neon-colored stems will stain your cutting board and other ingredients with which they're cooked. The best Swiss chard is found in cold-weather months; look for fresh, glossy bunches. A voluminous 1-pound bunch might look as if it could feed your whole neighborhood, but it will shrink when cooked to feed about four as a side dish.

Chard turns silky when blanched or simmered; it's delicious in stews and gratins. For a simple side dish, slice the leaves into ribbons, dice the stems, and braise both together with olive oil, chopped garlic, a pinch of chili powder, and a little chicken broth, until the stems are tender, about 20 minutes.

Baby Spinach with
SCALLIONS & LEMONS

SERVES 6

This recipe is very forgiving and keeps while sitting in the pan on the stove until you're ready to reheat it and serve.

- 2½ pounds baby spinach
- 3 tablespoons olive oil
- 4 scallions, trimmed and sliced, white and green parts kept separated

- Kosher salt and freshly ground black pepper
- 1 tablespoon lightly packed finely grated lemon zest (from about 1 large lemon)
- ⅛ teaspoon freshly grated nutmeg

Rinse and drain the spinach. (You needn't dry it completely; clinging droplets of water are fine.) Heat the oil in a large, deep Dutch oven or wok over medium heat. Add the scallion whites and cook, stirring, until they start to soften, about 1 minute. Pile in the spinach and cook, turning with tongs so it gets evenly heated. (You'll need to add the spinach in stages; as it heats, it will shrink.) Once all the spinach is in the pan, cover and cook, stirring occasionally, until all the leaves have wilted and released their liquid, about 2 minutes.

Uncover the pan, increase the heat to high, and cook, stirring occasionally, until the spinach is very soft, about 5 minutes. Remove from the heat and season with salt and pepper to taste. Just before serving, reheat gently, adding the scallion greens, lemon zest, and nutmeg. Drain briefly in a colander before serving. —RANDALL PRICE

Sautéed Asparagus with
BUTTER & PARMESAN

This simple and delicious side dish needs to be served soon after it's made, but you can get a jump on things by cutting the asparagus, chopping the parsley, and grating the cheese a few hours ahead. Once everything's prepped, the dish comes together in just minutes.

1½ pounds asparagus, trimmed

3 tablespoons unsalted butter

½ teaspoon kosher salt

¼ teaspoon freshly ground black pepper

1 tablespoon minced fresh flat-leaf parsley

¼ cup freshly grated Parmigiano-Reggiano

Trim the asparagus bottoms and then slice the spears on a sharp diagonal about ½ inch thick, leaving the tips whole. Melt the butter in a 12-inch skillet over medium heat. Add the asparagus and season with the salt and pepper. Cook, stirring often, until the asparagus is just tender, 5 to 6 minutes, lowering the heat if needed to keep it from browning. Don't overcook; the asparagus will soften a little more as it cools.

Remove the pan from the heat. Stir in the parsley and 3 tablespoons of the cheese. Transfer to a serving bowl, top with the remaining 1 tablespoon cheese, and serve immediately. —JANET FLETCHER

Braised Asparagus & Cipolline Onions
WITH PANCETTA & BALSAMIC BUTTER GLAZE

SERVES
3 TO 4

Browning the vegetables first and then simmering briefly to finish gives them the sweet caramelized flavor of a sauté and the pleasing texture and more complex flavor of a braise. This isn't the kind of dish that you can prepare in the morning and then reheat—the asparagus may get mushy—but you can make it and keep it warm for 30 minutes or so before dinner. To double the recipe, use two pans.

1 pound medium or thick asparagus

2 teaspoons balsamic vinegar

2 teaspoons fresh lemon juice

1 teaspoon Dijon mustard

1 teaspoon honey

2 tablespoons extra-virgin olive oil

1½ ounces thinly sliced pancetta, cut into slivers (about ⅓ cup)

1 tablespoon plus 1 teaspoon unsalted butter

5 ounces small cipolline onions (about 6) or large shallots (about 6), halved and peeled (quartered if very large)

Kosher salt

⅓ cup homemade or low-salt chicken broth

Cut off the tough ends of the asparagus so that all the spears are 6 to 7 inches long. Combine the vinegar, lemon juice, Dijon, and honey in a small bowl; set aside.

Heat 1 tablespoon of the oil in a 10-inch straight-sided sauté pan over medium-high heat. Add the pancetta strips and cook, stirring frequently, until browned and crisp, 2 to 3 minutes (don't let them burn). Take the pan off the heat and transfer the pancetta to a plate, leaving behind as much fat as possible. Return the pan to medium-high heat, add 1 tablespoon of the butter to the fat in the pan, and swirl to melt (there will be browned bits on the bottom of the pan). Add the onions and a pinch of salt and sauté until nicely browned on all sides and beginning to soften, 2 to 3 minutes. Take the pan off the heat and transfer the onions to another plate.

Return the pan to medium-high heat and add the remaining 1 tablespoon olive oil, the asparagus, and ¼ teaspoon salt. Toss well with tongs. Cook without stirring until the bottoms of the spears are nicely browned, 3 to 4 minutes. Toss, turn over, and cook for another 1 to 2 minutes to lightly brown another side. Return the onions to the pan, stir, and pour over the broth. Immediately cover the pan and simmer until the liquid is almost completely reduced, about 3 minutes.

Uncover, add the vinegar mixture, stir to coat thoroughly, and cook for a few seconds until it has a glazy consistency. Add the remaining 1 teaspoon butter and toss to melt and combine, scraping up any browned bits from the bottom of the pan. Toss in the crisped pancetta. Serve right away as individual servings or scrape the contents of the pan onto a small platter and serve family style. —SUSIE MIDDLETON

Browned Brussels Sprouts
WITH HAZELNUTS & LEMON

SERVES 8

You'll definitely want to toast, skin, and chop the nuts ahead of time; they'll hold just fine in an airtight container for a couple of days, or in the freezer for weeks.

½ cup hazelnuts

2 tablespoons olive oil

2 tablespoons unsalted butter

2 pounds fresh Brussels sprouts, trimmed and quartered

Kosher salt

¼ cup water

2 to 4 tablespoons fresh lemon juice

Freshly ground black pepper

Toast the nuts on a baking sheet in a heated 350°F oven, stirring occasionally, until very fragrant and the skins are deep brown and cracked, about 15 minutes. Wrap the nuts in a clean dishtowel (one you don't mind staining) and let steam for at least 5 minutes. Vigorously rub the nuts against one another in the towel to scrape off the skins (you won't get them all; aim for about half). Chop the nuts coarsely.

Heat a 12-inch skillet over medium-high heat. When it's hot, add the oil and butter. As soon as the butter melts, add the Brussels sprouts and spread evenly around the pan. Sprinkle with salt and cook without disturbing until browned on the first side, about 3 minutes. Continue to cook, stirring the sprouts occasionally, until they're well browned all over, another 5 to 8 minutes. Add the water, cover partially, and cook until tender, another 4 to 5 minutes (if the water evaporates completely during cooking, add more, 2 tablespoons at a time). Don't overcook; the sprouts shouldn't be mushy. Add the nuts. Season to taste with the lemon juice, salt, and pepper. Serve immediately or keep warm for up to 20 minutes. —DIANE MORGAN

HOW TO TRIM BRUSSELS SPROUTS

There isn't much mystery to trimming Brussels sprouts,
especially if you think of them as tiny cabbages with edible cores.

Trim the base of the core to expose a fresh surface.

Peel off and discard the outer layer of leaves, or more if necessary due to insect damage. Rinse the sprouts well.

If cooking the sprouts whole, score an X in the base of the core; this helps heat to penetrate the core so the sprouts cook evenly.

Slow-Cooked Broccoli with
GARLIC & PANCETTA

SERVES 4 TO 6; TO
DOUBLE THE RECIPE,
USE TWO PANS

This method is like a low-heat sauté; the broccoli cooks slowly in oil and becomes browned and deeply flavorful. Choose the largest skillet you have (the more surface area, the better), be sure to stir occasionally, and keep the heat low to prevent scorching. Before serving, give the dish a minute or two to cool; slow-cooked broccoli tastes better when it's not hot out of the pan—a boon to the Thanksgiving chef.

- 1¼ to 1½ pounds broccoli (about 1 bunch)
- ¼ cup extra-virgin olive oil
- 3 ounces pancetta, sliced ¼ inch thick and cut crosswise into ¼-inch-wide pieces (½ cup)
- 8 medium cloves garlic, thinly sliced
- ¾ teaspoon kosher salt; more to taste
- ¼ teaspoon crushed red pepper flakes

Tear off any broccoli leaves and trim the bottoms of the stems. Cut the florets just above where they join the large stem and then cut each floret through its stem (but not the buds) so that each piece is about ¼ inch thick at the stem end. Using a vegetable peeler or paring knife, peel the tough outer skin from the large stem, removing as little flesh as possible. Cut the stem into baton-shaped pieces about ¼ inch wide and 2 inches long.

Heat the oil in a 12-inch skillet over medium heat. Add the pancetta and cook until it's translucent and just starting to render its fat, about 2 minutes. Add the broccoli, garlic, salt, and red pepper flakes; stir to combine. Reduce the heat to medium low and cook, uncovered, stirring every 5 to 10 minutes, until the broccoli is tender and slightly browned, about 45 minutes total. Taste and add more salt, if necessary. Let cool briefly and serve.

—TASHA DESERIO

MUSHROOM & ROASTED GARLIC
"Succotash"

SERVES 10

You can use all button mushrooms or a mix, including shiitake, cremini, and your favorite wild mushrooms. You can make this updated Southern classic a day ahead and gently reheat it just before serving.

1 head garlic

1 tablespoon olive oil

2 slices bacon, chopped

1½ cups chopped onion

1 tablespoon finely chopped garlic

6 cups sliced fresh mushrooms (about 1 pound)

1 cup homemade or low-salt chicken broth

½ cup seeded and finely chopped red bell pepper

3 cups (about 13 ounces) frozen lima beans, thawed

2 teaspoons chopped fresh rosemary

Kosher salt and freshly ground black pepper

Heat the oven to 400°F. Cut off the top third of the head of garlic to expose the cloves. Coat the cut side with the oil. Wrap the garlic loosely in foil, put it on a baking sheet, and roast until very soft, about 1 hour. When cool enough to handle, squeeze out the soft garlic; set aside.

In a large skillet over medium-high heat, cook the bacon until crisp. Add the onion and chopped garlic and sauté until softened, about 2 minutes. Add the mushrooms and sauté until softened and lightly browned. Add the broth, roasted garlic, red pepper, and lima beans; cook until the beans are tender and the liquid is reduced, about 10 minutes. Add the rosemary; season with salt and pepper.

—ROBERT CARTER

Pearl Onion Gratin
WITH PARMESAN, SAVORY & THYME

SERVES 8

This is a delicious update of the traditional creamed onion dish that for some families is de rigueur *at Thanksgiving. Using frozen pearl onions saves lots of time and anguish, making this an easy side dish to pull together.*

2 pounds frozen pearl onions, thawed

¾ cup water

1 cup heavy cream

Three 4-inch sprigs fresh thyme

Kosher salt and freshly ground black pepper

3 tablespoons unsalted butter, melted

1 cup coarse fresh breadcrumbs

¼ cup freshly, finely grated Parmigiano-Reggiano

½ teaspoon dried savory, crumbled

Heat the oven to 400°F. Put the onions and water in a large saucepan over high heat. Stir and separate the onions with a fork as they heat. When the water boils, reduce the heat to medium, cover, and simmer for 5 minutes. Drain the onions well and pat dry.

Combine the cream, thyme, and ½ teaspoon salt in a small saucepan over medium-high heat. When the cream comes to a boil, reduce the heat to a simmer and cook for 5 minutes, stirring occasionally.

Meanwhile, brush a shallow 2-quart gratin or baking dish with 1 tablespoon of the butter. In a small bowl, toss the breadcrumbs, Parmigiano, savory, the remaining 2 tablespoons melted butter, ½ teaspoon salt, and several grinds of pepper.

Spread the onions in the baking dish. Pick out and discard the thyme sprigs from the cream. Pour the cream over the onions and scatter the breadcrumbs on top. Bake until the breadcrumbs are deep golden brown and the cream is bubbling furiously around the edges, about 30 minutes. Let rest for 10 minutes before serving. —JENNIFER ARMENTROUT

Roasted Onions
STUFFED WITH PROSCIUTTO & PARMESAN

One of these golden, savory onions makes a beautiful side dish to roast turkey; you could even serve this as a starter, on a bed of spicy salad greens. You can bake and scoop the onions a day ahead of time and then fill and reheat them right before dinner, but do allow some time for them to cool a bit; they're best warm, not hot.

8 medium onions

¼ cup olive oil

2½ cups dry white wine

Table salt and freshly ground black pepper

4 sprigs fresh thyme

1⅓ cups dry fresh breadcrumbs

1 cup grated Parmigiano-Reggiano

½ pound thinly sliced prosciutto, coarsely chopped

¼ cup heavy cream

1 tablespoon chopped fresh thyme

2 tablespoons chopped fresh flat-leaf parsley

Heat the oven to 425°F. Slice off the top quarter of the onions. Peel them and trim the bottoms just enough to make them sit flat.

Heat the oil in a large, heavy-based ovenproof skillet until hot. Put the onions, cut side down, in the pan and cook just the cut side until well browned, about 5 minutes. (Do this in two batches if necessary to avoid crowding.) Take the pan off the heat. Turn the onions cut side up and pour the wine over them. Sprinkle with salt and pepper. Add the thyme sprigs to the pan and bake the onions until just tender when poked with a knife, about 1 hour.

Remove the onions from the skillet (reserving the liquid in the pan) and let cool slightly. With a spoon, scoop out the inside of each onion, leaving a rim ¼ to ½ inch thick (about two layers of onion). Chop enough of the scooped-out onion to make about ⅓ cup.

In a medium bowl, mix the chopped onion with the breadcrumbs, Parmigiano, prosciutto, cream, chopped thyme, and parsley. Season with salt and pepper. Divide the filling among the hollowed onions, return the onions to the skillet with the liquid, and put back in the oven. Bake until the onions are very tender and the filling is hot, about 20 minutes. Serve with some of the pan juices spooned over the onions. —GORDON HAMERSLEY

Roasted Winter Vegetables with a
MAPLE-GINGER GLAZE

SERVES 8

Thin matchsticks of ginger roast along with the vegetables, absorbing the butter and maple syrup so that they caramelize and become soft, chewy, and irresistible. Some minced ginger is also tossed in at the end to add a fresh, sharp finishing note. These vegetables don't need to be served piping hot; they're happy to stay in a warm spot, lightly covered, while you finish up the turkey gravy.

1 pound parsnips, peeled and cut into 2x½-inch sticks

1 pound carrots, peeled and cut into 2x½-inch sticks

1 pound turnips, peeled and cut into thin wedges

1 pound Brussels sprouts, trimmed (see How to Trim Brussels Sprouts, page 109) and any wilted leaves pulled off; large sprouts halved

One 4-inch piece fresh ginger, peeled and sliced into very thin matchsticks (about ⅔ cup)

6 tablespoons (¾ stick) unsalted butter, melted

Kosher salt and freshly ground black pepper

2 teaspoons peeled and grated fresh ginger

3 tablespoons pure maple syrup

Heat the oven to 425°F. Spread the vegetables and the ginger matchsticks in two large, low-sided roasting pans or heavy rimmed baking sheets. Drizzle with the butter and season with salt and pepper. Toss to evenly coat the vegetables and spread them so that they're just one layer deep. Roast them, tossing a couple of times, until tender and golden brown in spots, about 30 minutes.

In a small bowl, combine the grated ginger and maple syrup, then drizzle over the vegetables, toss to coat, and roast for another 5 minutes. The vegetables should be very tender and browned in spots. Serve warm. — EVA KATZ

CLASSIC
Glazed Carrots

The herbs add a fresh touch to this traditional and somewhat sweet side dish. Get a jump on the prep by peeling, trimming, and cutting the carrots the day before; store them in a zip-top plastic bag in the fridge. You can easily double the recipe, but either use two pans or cook the carrots in batches, reheating the first batch just before serving.

1½ pounds carrots (about 8), peeled and trimmed

About 1 cup water

2 tablespoons unsalted butter

1 tablespoon granulated sugar

1 teaspoon kosher salt; more as needed

1½ tablespoons chopped fresh flat-leaf parsley, chervil, or chives (optional)

Cut the carrots in half lengthwise. Holding your knife at a sharp angle, cut the halves into 2-inch lengths to make diamond shapes; try to make all the pieces the same size so they cook evenly. Put the carrots in a 10- to 12-inch sauté pan (they should be almost in a single layer) and add enough water to come halfway up the sides of the carrots. Add the butter, sugar, and salt, and bring to a boil over high heat. Cover the pan with the lid slightly askew, reduce the heat to medium high, and cook at a steady boil, shaking the pan occasionally, until the carrots are tender but not soft (a paring knife should enter a carrot with just a little resistance), 12 to 14 minutes.

Uncover and continue to boil until the liquid evaporates and a syrup forms. Shake the pan and roll the pieces around to evenly glaze the carrots. Taste and add a pinch more salt if necessary. Toss with the fresh herbs and serve.

— TASHA DESERIO

FOUR WAYS TO CUT A CARROT

Carrots are a fun vegetable to work with because of the many ways you can cut them. For glazing, you can use just about any cut you want, as long as the pieces are about the same size and shape, which helps them cook evenly. It's easier to accomplish this if you start with whole carrots that are all about the same width, and if they're more cylindrical than conical; carrots with wide tops and thin tips are tricky to cut evenly.

OVAL SLICES Cut the carrot into ¼-inch-thick oval slices with a sharp diagonal cut (on the bias).

DIAMONDS Cut the carrot in half lengthwise. Cut the halves into 1- or 2-inch lengths (measured point to point) with a sharp diagonal cut.

ROLL CUT Trim the tip of the carrot with a sharp diagonal cut. Roll the carrot 180 degrees and cut off a 1-inch piece, keeping your knife at the same diagonal angle as the original cut. Continue to roll and cut the carrot in this way.

HALF MOONS Cut the carrot in half lengthwise. Cut each half into ¼-inch-thick slices with a sharp diagonal cut.

MAPLE-GLAZED
Carrots | SERVES 4 TO 6

Pure maple syrup is essential, so don't grab the kids' pancake syrup. The recipe calls for the roll cut (see page 117), which is a useful cut to know. You can cut the carrots in whatever shape you like, however; just be sure the pieces are all about the same size, for even cooking. You can easily double the recipe, but either use two pans or cook the carrots in batches, reheating the first batch just before serving.

1½ pounds carrots (about 8), peeled and trimmed

About 1 cup water

2 tablespoons unsalted butter

1½ tablespoons pure maple syrup

1 teaspoon kosher salt; more as needed

Cut the carrots using the roll cut (see page 17). Put the carrots in a 10- to 12-inch sauté pan (they should be almost in a single layer) and add enough water to come halfway up the sides of the carrots. Add the butter, maple syrup, and salt, and bring to a boil over high heat. Cover the pan with the lid slightly askew, reduce the heat to medium high, and cook at a steady boil, shaking the pan occasionally, until the carrots are tender but not soft (a paring knife should enter a carrot with just a little resistance), about 10 minutes.

Uncover and continue to boil until the liquid evaporates, a syrup forms, and the carrots start to caramelize and become lightly tinged with brown. Shake the pan and roll the pieces around to evenly glaze. Taste, add a pinch of salt, if needed, and serve. —TASHA DESERIO

Roasted Carrots & Parsnips with
SHALLOT & HERB BUTTER

You can cut and oil the vegetables up to one day ahead, but don't add the salt because it will draw out moisture from them. The shallot and herb butter adds a zesty finish; you can add crunch by tossing on a handful of toasted pine nuts, too.

10 large carrots (about 2 pounds)

8 large parsnips (about 2 pounds)

6 tablespoons extra-virgin olive oil

2 teaspoons kosher salt; more to taste

¾ teaspoon freshly ground black pepper; more to taste

½ cup (1 stick) unsalted butter, softened

¼ cup minced shallots

¼ cup finely chopped fresh chives

1 tablespoon finely chopped fresh rosemary

1 tablespoon chopped fresh thyme

1 large clove garlic, minced

Position racks in the top and bottom thirds of the oven and heat the oven to 450°F.

Peel and cut the carrots and parsnips into 2x¼-inch matchsticks. Put them in a large bowl; toss with the oil. Sprinkle with the salt and pepper and toss again. Transfer the vegetables to two 10x15-inch Pyrex® baking dishes, dividing the vegetables evenly, and roast, stirring every 15 minutes, until they are nicely browned, 40 to 45 minutes. For even browning, swap the positions of the dishes after 30 minutes.

Meanwhile, combine the butter, shallot, herbs, and garlic in a small bowl and stir well. When the vegetables come out of the oven, combine them in a serving dish. Add the butter and toss to coat. Serve immediately. —JULIANNA GRIMES

IS THAT A WHITE CARROT?

The parsnip is an ivory-colored root vegetable, similar in shape to the carrot, but slightly rougher in texture; it can reach almost a foot long. At the market, parsnips should be firm and crisp, never rubbery. Peel their thin skins as you would a carrot's, but only eat parsnips cooked, which turns the flesh moist, sweet, and nutty.

Butternut Squash, Apple, Leek &
Potato Gratin WITH A CHEDDAR CRUST

SERVES 8

*You can assemble this wonderful holiday dish earlier in the day and then bake it as you're pull-
ing dinner together. Be sure the leeks and apples are cool before combining them with the other
ingredients in the gratin dish. Refrigerate the assembled gratin without the topping and remove it
from the fridge 45 minutes before baking. Sprinkle a spoonful or two of chicken or vegetable broth
over the top if you've made this several hours ahead, then, just before popping it in the oven, add the
crumb topping.*

FOR THE TOPPING:

1½ cups coarse fresh breadcrumbs (from an airy, crusty loaf like ciabatta)

2 tablespoons unsalted butter, melted

Kosher salt

¾ cup (3 ounces) grated sharp Cheddar

1 teaspoon fresh thyme leaves

FOR THE GRATIN:

¼ cup (½ stick) unsalted butter, plus ½ teaspoon for the dish

2 cups sliced leeks (white and light green parts of 3 medium leeks), thoroughly rinsed

Kosher salt

⅔ cup plus 3 tablespoons apple cider

½ cup plus 3 tablespoons heavy cream

2 teaspoons chopped fresh thyme leaves

Freshly ground black pepper

2 crisp, firm apples, such as Golden Delicious or Braeburn, peeled, cored, and thinly sliced

¾ pound butternut squash (from the neck of the squash)

2 medium Yukon Gold potatoes

MAKE THE TOPPING: Combine the crumbs, melted butter, and a pinch of salt in a bowl.
Mix in the Cheddar and thyme leaves and set aside.

MAKE THE GRATIN: Heat the oven to 350°F. Rub a shallow 2-quart gratin dish with
½ teaspoon of the butter. Melt the remaining 2 tablespoons butter in a small (preferably
nonstick) saucepan over medium heat. Add the leeks and a big pinch of salt. Cook, stirring
frequently, until well softened and lightly browned (the pan will be dry), 10 to 15 minutes.
Add ⅔ cup of the cider and simmer for 2 minutes to reduce it slightly. Add ½ cup of the
cream, the chopped thyme, a pinch of salt, a few grinds of pepper, and stir well; set aside.

In a large nonstick skillet, melt the remaining 2 tablespoons butter over medium heat.
Turn the heat to medium high, add the apple slices, and cook, gently flipping and stirring,
until browned and limp but not falling apart, about 10 minutes. Add the remaining 3 tablespoons each cream and cider. Stir and let the liquid reduce slightly for a few seconds; remove
from the heat.

Peel the squash neck, cut it into quarters lengthwise, and cut them across into thin slices. Peel the potatoes, cut them in half, and then cut them across into thin half-moons. In a large bowl, combine the squash, potatoes, the leek mixture, apple mixture (scrape the pans well), and a scant 2 teaspoons salt. Using a rubber spatula, mix gently but thoroughly. Scrape the mixture into the prepared gratin dish, smoothing and pressing until evenly distributed. Cover evenly with the breadcrumb topping.

Bake until the crust is deep golden brown, the juices around the edges have subsided, and the crust is dark brown around the edges, about 1 hour. Let rest for 15 to 20 minutes before serving. —SUSIE MIDDLETON

BUTTERNUT IS THE DARLING OF THE WINTER SQUASH FAMILY

Of all the colorful and flavorful winter squashes available around Thanksgiving, butternut squash is perhaps the most versatile and

delicious, and easiest to handle. While you'll need a sharp paring knife or a good peeler (a Y peeler works well) to get through the tough skin, it's a lot easier to peel the smooth butternut than it is one of the fluted squash varieties. A butternut also has a long neck section of seedless flesh that allows you to cut evenly shaped slices for gratins. The flesh of a butternut is finely grained, bright orange, and has a rich, sweet flavor. Be sure to thoroughly cook the squash so it's tender, but not to the point of mushiness.

5

Potatoes
& Grains

There's mashed potatoes, of course (and we've got a half dozen of the best), but this year, you can explore beyond the fluffy side to other potato dishes, such as crusty-creamy herb-roasted potatoes and layered potato gratins, which are graciously do-ahead. And don't stop with the spud—sweet potatoes and nutty grains also pair beautifully with turkey and are perfect for soaking up the gravy.

ULTIMATE
Fluffy Mashed Potatoes

SERVES 4 TO 6; THE RECIPE CAN BE DOUBLED

For the fluffiest mashed potatoes, russets are your best choice because of their high starch content. For the ultimate luxurious texture, use a ricer, though these rich potatoes are still delicious made with a hand masher. The crème fraîche adds a nice tang, but if you can't find it (many supermarkets carry it in the specialty cheese section), use a mix of heavy cream and sour cream. You can make mashed potatoes ahead of time and gently reheat them over low heat, in a double boiler, or very carefully in the microwave. You may need to stir in a little more liquid to loosen the consistency.

1¾ to 2 pounds russet potatoes, peeled and cut into large chunks (1½ to 2 inches)

Kosher salt

1 cup crème fraîche (or ½ cup heavy cream plus ½ cup sour cream)

1 teaspoon grated lemon zest

2 tablespoons unsalted butter, softened

Freshly ground white pepper

Put the potatoes in a large saucepan and cover with cold water by at least an inch. Add a generous ½ teaspoon salt and bring to a boil. Lower the heat to maintain a steady simmer, cover the pot partially, and cook until the potatoes are quite tender when tested with a metal skewer, 15 to 20 minutes.

Meanwhile, heat the crème fraîche (or heavy cream and sour cream) in a small saucepan over low heat, stirring occasionally, until smooth and just hot. Set aside in a warm spot.

Drain the potatoes, dump them back into the pan, and dry them over low heat, shaking the pan and stirring until the potatoes look floury and leave a light film on the bottom of the pan. If using a ricer, dump the potatoes into a bowl and rice them back into the pot set over very low heat. If using a hand masher, mash them in the pot until completely smooth.

Using a wooden spoon, beat in the lemon zest and butter. Add the crème fraîche, about ¼ cup at a time, beating well after each addition. Season with salt and pepper and serve right away, or reheat gently over low heat, adding a little milk to loosen if necessary.
—ROY FINAMORE & MOLLY STEVENS

TIPS FOR BETTER MASHED POTATOES

ᔨ Start the potatoes in cold water and bring to a simmer, which allows them to cook evenly.

ᔨ Simmer the potatoes gently. If they boil too violently, they'll fall apart before they're cooked.

ᔨ Test for doneness with a metal skewer. It's more accurate than a knife and less damaging than a fork.

ᔨ After cooking, drain thoroughly, shaking to rid the potatoes of excess water; return them to the pot over low heat and stir to dry them fully.

ᔨ The best tool for mashing is a ricer, but you can also use a food mill or a potato masher.

ᔨ Never use a food processor to mash russets; you'll overwork them and give them a gluey texture.

Purée of Yukon Gold Potatoes WITH PARMESAN

Yukon Golds are nice, medium-starch potatoes that give you rich flavor and a dense but creamy texture. The Parmesan adds just a hint of tang, and blends beautifully with mild turkey and rich gravy of any kind. To save time, grate the cheese a day ahead and keep it tightly sealed in the refrigerator.

8 large Yukon Gold potatoes (3½ to 4 pounds total), peeled, quartered, and rinsed

Kosher salt

1½ cups milk; more if needed

½ cup heavy cream

½ cup (1 stick) unsalted butter, softened

½ cup freshly grated Parmigiano-Reggiano

Freshly ground black pepper

Put the quartered potatoes in a large saucepan with enough cold water to cover. Partially cover the pot and bring to a boil. Uncover, add 2 teaspoons salt, and reduce the heat so the water boils gently. Cook until the potatoes are tender when pierced with a fork, 10 to 12 minutes.

Meanwhile, heat the milk and cream together on the stovetop or in a microwave until hot but not boiling.

Drain the potatoes, return them to the pan, and dry them over low heat, shaking the pan and stirring until they look floury and leave a light film on the bottom of the pan. If using a ricer, dump the potatoes into a bowl and rice them back into the pot set over very low heat. If using a hand masher, mash them in the pot until completely smooth.

Blend in the butter and Parmigiano. Gradually add the milk mixture until the purée is as soft and moist as you like. Season with salt and pepper to taste. —DIANE MORGAN

Tip

If you're not serving them right away, keep your mashed potatoes warm in the top of a double boiler (or in a heatproof bowl set over a pan of simmering water).

Smashed Red-Skinned Potatoes
WITH BOURSIN & SCALLIONS

Don't we all know someone who loves lumps? This is the perfect dish for them, and for anyone who'll enjoy the fresh herby, garlicky flavor. If you can find it, try substituting Gorgonzola dolce for the Boursin. Be sure not to overwork the potatoes or they may turn gummy. You can keep these potatoes for 20 minutes or so in a warmed dish, covered with foil, or in a low oven, but they're not the best candidates for make-ahead and reheating.

1¾ to 2 pounds red-skinned potatoes, scrubbed and cut into large chunks (1½ to 2 inches)

Kosher salt

2 tablespoons unsalted butter, softened, cut into pieces

¼ pound Boursin cheese (with garlic and herbs), at room temperature, cut into pieces

3 scallions (white parts with some green), chopped

Freshly ground black pepper

Put the potatoes in a large saucepan and cover with cold water by at least an inch. Add a generous ½ teaspoon salt and bring to a boil. Lower the heat to maintain a steady simmer, cover the pot partially, and cook until the potatoes are quite tender when tested with a metal skewer, 15 to 20 minutes. Drain the potatoes—reserving some of the cooking water—and dump them back in the pot. Dry the potatoes over medium heat, shaking the pan and stirring, until most of the moisture has steamed off. Reduce the heat to very low.

Use the side of a big metal spoon to cut through the skins and flesh of the potatoes, reducing the chunks to a very coarse mash.

Stir in the butter and then the Boursin. If you want, loosen the mash with cooking water: Depending on the potatoes, you might need a few tablespoons or as much as ½ cup. Don't beat vigorously or the potatoes may turn gummy. Stir in the scallions, add salt and pepper to taste, and serve right away. —ROY FINAMORE & MOLLY STEVENS

CLASSIC
Roasted Potatoes
SERVES 4 TO 6

Roasted potatoes are a wonderful crisp alternative to mashed. This recipe can easily be scaled up or down according to how many mouths you're feeding. If you double it, use two pans. To make roasted potatoes ahead, just keep them in foil and reheat in a 375°F oven; they may not be as crisp as when first roasted. Take care to not let them dry out.

2 pounds waxy potatoes, left whole if very small, halved or cut into chunks if large

3 tablespoons olive oil, melted butter, or duck fat

2 tablespoons chopped fresh thyme or rosemary (optional)

1 teaspoon kosher salt

Plenty of freshly ground black pepper

3 tablespoons mixed chopped fresh tender herbs (choose from parsley, chives, chervil, dill, mint)

Juice of 1 lemon

Heat the oven to 375°F. Spread the potatoes in a single layer in a medium roasting pan or rimmed baking sheet. Drizzle with the oil, season with the thyme or rosemary, salt, and pepper, and toss to coat well. Roast, tossing with a metal spatula a few times to prevent sticking, until the potatoes are very tender throughout and the skins are somewhat shriveled and crisp, 50 to 60 minutes, depending on their size and variety.

As soon as the potatoes are done, toss with chopped tender herbs and drizzle with the lemon juice to taste. Serve hot. — MOLLY STEVENS

Red Potato Slices with
LEMON & OLIVES

SERVES 6

Add some Mediterranean zest to your American holiday table with these roasted potatoes. The sliced lemons look so pretty in this festive dish. To get ahead, cut the lemons, mince the garlic, and chop the parsley earlier in the day and refrigerate.

2 pounds medium or large red-skinned potatoes, scrubbed and sliced ¼ inch thick

3 tablespoons olive oil; more for the pan

1 lemon, very thinly sliced (discard the ends and seeds)

2 cloves garlic, minced

¼ cup chopped fresh flat-leaf parsley

1½ teaspoons kosher salt

¼ teaspoon freshly ground black pepper

⅓ cup pitted oil-cured olives (optional)

Position a rack in the middle of the oven and heat the oven to 425°F. Generously oil a large baking dish (9x13-inch works well, or use an oval gratin dish).

In a large bowl, combine the potatoes, oil, lemon slices, garlic, parsley, salt, and pepper; toss well. Spread the mixture in the baking dish so the potatoes are evenly layered (it can be rustic looking). Roast, turning with a metal spatula every 20 minutes, until most of the potatoes are crisp and golden and the lemon skins are shriveled and caramelized, about 1 hour. Scatter over the olives, if using, for the last 3 to 5 minutes of cooking. —EVA KATZ

Red Potatoes
WITH ONIONS, THYME & SHERRY VINEGAR

SERVES 6

These potatoes are a sophisticated change of pace. They're best when served shortly after roasting, so to get ahead, you can toss everything together in a bowl—except the salt—up to 6 hours before dinner. (Adding the salt ahead can make the vegetables weep liquid.) When ready to roast (perhaps while the turkey's resting and you're making gravy), add the salt, spread the potatoes on the baking sheet, and roast.

2 small red onions

2 pounds very small red-skinned potatoes (about 20), scrubbed and halved

3 tablespoons olive oil

3 tablespoons sherry vinegar

Kosher salt and freshly ground black pepper

3 tablespoons fresh thyme leaves (from about 1 bunch)

Position a rack in the middle of the oven. Heat the oven to 425°F. Trim the root ends of the onions, leaving enough of the core intact to hold the onion wedges together. Trim the other end of the onions and cut the onions in half vertically. Cut each half into four wedges, about 1 inch wide.

In a medium bowl, combine the onions, potatoes, oil, and vinegar and season with salt and pepper. Toss to coat well. Spread the vegetables and any liquid in the bowl on a large rimmed baking sheet in a single layer, making sure the potatoes are all cut side down. Roast until the cut sides of the potatoes are crusty and golden brown, about 35 minutes. Turn the potatoes and onions using a metal spatula. Sprinkle the thyme over the top, return the pan to the oven, and roast until the potatoes are tender and the onions are very brown, about another 5 minutes. Taste and season with more salt if needed. —EVA KATZ

ROASTED
Potatoes & Turnips

SERVES 4 TO 6

Adding a bit of broth at the start of roasting gives these vegetables a creamier, softer texture than dry-roasting—more like potatoes that have been roasted alongside a hefty cut of meat. During roasting, the vegetables absorb the broth, and then begin to brown. Once you try this recipe, you might be surprised by how much you like turnips. The recipe can be doubled; use two pans.

3 small bay leaves

2 sprigs fresh thyme

1 pound yellow-fleshed potatoes, peeled and cut into 1½-inch chunks

1 pound turnips, peeled and quartered or cut into 1½-inch chunks

½ cup Quick But Rich Turkey Giblet Broth (page 56) or homemade or low-salt chicken broth or water

¼ cup (½ stick) unsalted butter, cut into 4 pieces

1 teaspoon kosher salt

Freshly ground black pepper

Heat the oven to 375°F. Put the bay leaves and thyme in the bottom of a large gratin dish or a medium roasting pan. Dump the potatoes and turnips on top. Pour in the broth and scatter the butter around. Season with the salt and pepper. Roast, tossing with a metal spatula a few times, until the vegetables are very tender and browned in spots, about 1 hour. Remove the thyme and bay leaves and serve hot. — MOLLY STEVENS

YUKON GOLD
Gruyère Galette

SERVES 4 TO 6

This nutty, cheesy potato dish is brilliant for the busy cook because it reheats beautifully. Bake the galette earlier in the day (or the day before). Let cool, then cut it into wedges. Arrange the wedges on a baking sheet and reheat, uncovered, at 350°F for about 15 minutes. Arrange the wedges on a platter or directly on the dinner plates. Make two or more for a crowd.

¼ cup finely chopped shallots (1 to 2 large shallots)

3 tablespoons extra-virgin olive oil; plus ½ teaspoon for the pan (or use olive-oil spray for the pan)

1 pound Yukon Gold potatoes (about 2 large or 3 medium), scrubbed and left unpeeled

1 heaping teaspoon very lightly chopped fresh thyme

Kosher salt

½ cup (1½ ounces) finely grated Parmigiano-Reggiano

1 cup (about 3½ ounces) finely grated Gruyère

Combine the shallots and 3 tablespoons of the oil in a small saucepan and bring to a simmer over medium heat. Reduce to a low simmer; cook the shallots until nicely softened (don't let them brown), about 2 minutes. Remove from the heat and let cool completely (about 25 minutes at room temperature; cool them more quickly in the refrigerator. if you like).

Heat the oven to 400°F. Rub the bottom and inside edge of a 7½-inch tart pan with a removable bottom with the remaining ½ teaspoon olive oil or coat with olive-oil spray. Put the pan on a rimmed baking sheet lined with foil.

Slice the potatoes as thinly as possible (about 1/16 inch) with a chef's knife. If the potato wobbles, slice a thin lengthwise sliver off the bottom to stabilize it; then continue slicing crosswise. Discard the ends. Put the potatoes in a large bowl, add the shallots and oil, along with the thyme and toss well to thoroughly coat the potatoes (a small rubber spatula works well).

Cover the bottom of the tart pan with a layer of potato slices, overlapping them slightly. Start along the outside edge of the pan and, making slightly overlapping rings, move inward until the bottom is covered with a layer of potatoes. Sprinkle the potatoes with salt (a generous ⅛ teaspoon), then sprinkle about one-quarter of the Parmigiano and about one-quarter of the Gruyère over all. Arrange another layer of potatoes, season with salt, sprinkle with cheese, and repeat two more times, until you have four layers of potatoes. (This is a messy job; you'll need a damp towel to wipe your hands between layers.) Top the last layer with more salt and any remaining cheese.

Bake the galette until the top is a reddish golden brown and the potatoes are tender in all places (a fork with thin tines should poke easily through all the layers), 45 to 50 minutes. The bottom will be crisp and the sides brown.

Let the galette cool for 10 or 15 minutes in the pan. It will then be cool enough to handle but still plenty hot inside for serving. Have a cutting board nearby. Run a paring knife around the edge of the galette to loosen it and carefully remove the tart ring by gently pressing the tart bottom up. Slide a very thin spatula under and all around the bottom layer to free it from the pan bottom. Use the spatula to gently slide the galette onto a cutting board. Cut into four or six wedges, or as many as you like. —SUSIE MIDDLETON

LAYERS OF SUCCESS

1 Start layering the herb-coated potato slices along the outside of the pan and work inward.

2 Sprinkle the first layer of potatoes with cheese and then arrange the next layer of potatoes.

3 The last layers will mound up a bit higher than the top edge of the pan.

4 A fully cooked golden galette recedes slightly from the top and sides of the pan.

CLASSIC
Potato Gratin | SERVES 6 TO 8

This is an excellent dish for a busy Thanksgiving cook because you can make it a day ahead and reheat it; it's almost better that way. However, you must reheat in very low heat or the fat in the cream will separate. Let the gratin come fully to room temperature (if it was refrigerated), then reheat for a few minutes at 325°F. It's also excellent at warm room temperature, so you could bake it in the morning and serve it as is for an afternoon Thanksgiving. Try to get a good-quality Gruyère or Emmental, which will be moderately assertive yet mellow and nutty.

2 pounds Yukon Gold or russet potatoes, peeled

3 cups whipping or heavy cream

1 teaspoon kosher salt

⅛ teaspoon freshly ground black pepper

Generous pinch of freshly grated nutmeg

2 cloves garlic, smashed and peeled

¾ cup finely shredded Gruyère, Emmental, or Comté

Heat the oven to 400°F.

Using a very sharp knife or a mandoline, carefully cut the potatoes into ⅛-inch-thick slices (no thicker). Put the potatoes in a large heavy-based saucepan and add the cream, salt, pepper, nutmeg, and garlic. Cook over medium-high heat until the cream is boiling, stirring occasionally (very gently with a rubber spatula so you don't break up the slices, but be sure to separate the slices).

When the cream boils, pour the mixture into a 2½- or 3-quart baking dish. If you don't want a tender but garlicky surprise mouthful, remove and discard the garlic cloves. Shake the dish a bit to let the slices settle and then sprinkle the surface with the cheese.

Bake until the top is deep golden brown, the cream has thickened, and the potatoes are extremely tender when pierced with a knife, about 40 minutes. Don't worry if the dish looks too liquidy at this point; it will set up as it cools a bit. Before serving, let the potatoes cool until they're very warm but not hot (at least 15 minutes) or serve them at room temperature. —MARTHA HOLMBERG

Tip

Gratins and galettes need even slices. To make that easier, cut a slice from the bottom of your potato so it sits firmly on the surface.

MOLASSES MASHED
Sweet Potatoes with Ginger

This mash is a great partner for roast turkey, but it also plays beautifully with pork and ham. The flavors are more complex and sophisticated than a typical mashed sweet potato, thanks to the carrots, parsnips, and judicious use of molasses and ginger. You can make this up to a day ahead and reheat it over gentle heat or in the microwave before serving.

4 medium sweet potatoes (2 pounds total), peeled and cut into 1-inch chunks

8 small carrots (1 pound total), peeled and cut into 1-inch chunks

4 medium parsnips (1 pound total), peeled and cut into 1-inch chunks

Kosher salt

¼ cup (½ stick) unsalted butter

¼ cup sour cream

¼ cup molasses

4 teaspoons peeled and grated fresh ginger

½ cup half-and-half

Freshly ground black pepper

In a large saucepan or soup pot, combine the sweet potatoes, carrots, and parsnips; cover with cold water. Bring to a boil, salt the water generously, and simmer until tender, 15 to 20 minutes. Drain and return to the saucepan. Set the pan over low heat, uncovered, and let the vegetables dry in the pan for about 2 minutes, shaking the pan occasionally so they don't stick.

Pass the vegetables through a food mill or mash them by hand, if you prefer. Stir in the butter, sour cream, molasses, ginger, and half-and-half (if you're preparing the potatoes ahead, save about ¼ cup of the half-and-half for reheating). Add about 1 teaspoon salt along with pepper to taste, adjust the seasonings, and serve.

—KAREN & BEN BARKER

Sweet Potato-Russet Potato Gratin
WITH HORSERADISH & A DIJON CRUST

SERVES 8

While the intrigue of this dish comes from the play between the sweetness of sweet potatoes and the tanginess of horseradish and mustard, the structure of the dish is helped by the russets, which have a sturdier slice.

FOR THE TOPPING:

1½ cups coarse fresh breadcrumbs (from an airy, crusty loaf like ciabatta)

2 tablespoons unsalted butter, melted

Kosher salt

1 tablespoon Dijon mustard

2 tablespoons freshly grated Parmigiano-Reggiano

2 teaspoons chopped fresh flat-leaf parsley

FOR THE GRATIN:

2 tablespoons plus ½ teaspoon unsalted butter

1 cup thinly sliced shallots (6 to 7 large shallots)

Kosher salt

⅔ cup heavy cream

⅔ cup homemade or low-salt chicken broth

2 tablespoons prepared horseradish

Freshly ground black pepper

1 large (12-ounce) russet potato

1 large (12-ounce) sweet potato

⅓ cup freshly grated Parmigiano-Reggiano

MAKE THE TOPPING: Combine the breadcrumbs, melted butter, and a pinch of salt in a bowl. Mix in the mustard and then the Parmigiano and parsley.

PREPARE THE GRATIN: Heat the oven to 350°F. Rub a shallow 2-quart gratin dish with ½ teaspoon of the butter.

Melt the remaining 2 tablespoons butter in a small saucepan over medium heat. Add the shallots and a big pinch of salt; cook, stirring frequently, until softened, limp, and somewhat golden. Whisk together the cream, broth, and horseradish; add to the shallots. Season with salt and pepper, stir to combine, and take off the heat.

Peel the potato and sweet potato, cut each in half lengthwise, and slice each across into thin half-moons. In a large bowl, combine them along with 2 teaspoons salt, the Parmigiano, and shallot cream. With a rubber spatula, mix gently but thoroughly and scrape into the prepared gratin dish, smoothing and pressing until evenly distributed. Cover with the breadcrumb topping.

Bake until the crust is deep golden brown, the juices around the edges have subsided, and the potatoes are tender when pierced with a fork, about 1 hour. Let rest for 15 to 20 minutes before serving. —SUSIE MIDDLETON

SWEET POTATOES VS. YAMS

SWEET POTATO

YAM

Cruise the potato section in most produce stores and you'll likely see a sign for yams above coppery colored, pointy root vegetables. Visit an Hispanic or Asian market and you'll find a decidedly different vegetable—with dark, rough, scaly skin—also labeled as a yam.

The truth is that the supermarket yam is not a yam at all, but a type of sweet potato.

The sweet potato is grown around the world, although it's indigenous to the Americas and is especially popular in the southern United States. According to the North Carolina Sweet Potato Commission, the naming confusion began decades ago when Louisiana farmers developed a new sweet potato with dark-orange flesh that's moister than the light-skinned, pale-fleshed sweet potatoes. To distinguish this new breed, they called it a yam and the name stuck. Today, the USDA requires that these "yams" (sometimes called American or Louisiana yams) also be correctly labeled as sweet potatoes.

The true yam is an unrelated species that's much starchier than the sweet potato and is a staple food for much of Latin America, Africa, and Asia. Called *ñame* or *igname*, it can be huge and irregularly shaped. The skin is usually pale to dark brown, and the crisp, dry flesh is white to ivory to yellow. Yams taste rather bland and they aren't sweet.

SWEET POTATO & GRITS
Spoon Bread

SERVES 12

Technically, spoon bread is made with cornmeal, but in this recipe, country-style grits add wonderful texture. Instant grits and even polenta will also give the dish good corn flavor and texture. If using one of these substitutions, follow the package directions for cooking times.

FOR THE SWEET POTATOES:

2 pounds sweet potatoes, peeled and cut into 1-inch chunks

2½ teaspoons kosher salt

½ teaspoon freshly ground white pepper

¼ teaspoon ground nutmeg

¼ teaspoon ground cinnamon

½ cup pure maple syrup

3 large eggs, separated

FOR THE GRITS:

3 cups water

½ teaspoon chopped garlic

2 tablespoons unsalted butter

½ teaspoon kosher salt

Pinch cayenne (optional)

1¼ cups stone-ground grits

2 tablespoons heavy cream

COOK THE SWEET POTATOES: Put the sweet potatoes in a large pot; cover with water and add 1½ teaspoons of the salt. Bring to a boil, reduce the heat, and simmer until the potatoes are fork-tender, about 10 minutes. Drain and purée the potatoes in a food mill or ricer. Fold in the remaining 1 teaspoon salt, the white pepper, nutmeg, cinnamon, and maple syrup. Set aside.

WHILE THE POTATOES BOIL, COOK THE GRITS: In a medium, heavy-based pot, bring the water and garlic to a boil. Add the butter, salt, and cayenne. Gradually whisk in the grits. Bring to a boil, reduce the heat, and simmer, stirring occasionally, until the grits are cooked and creamy and just start to pull away from the side of the pot, about 30 minutes. Remove from the heat and fold in the cream.

Heat the oven to 400°F. In a large bowl, mix the sweet potato purée with the grits. Mix in the egg yolks. In a separate bowl, with a whisk or electric mixer, whisk the egg whites until they form soft peaks; gently fold into the sweet potatoes. Spread in a 9x13-inch casserole and bake until the pudding sets and the top is lightly browned, about 35 minutes. Serve hot or warm. —ROBERT CARTER

Tip

Cook the grits until they're creamy and just begin to come away from the sides of the pot. You should still be able to see individual grains in the grits.

Wild Rice with
DRIED CRANBERRIES & HAZELNUTS

SERVES 6 TO 8

Unlike long-grain white rice, wild rice has no set cooking time or ratio of water to rice. You can tell it's done when most of the grains have "popped"—split open to reveal a creamy interior, ends curling slightly. You can cook the rice up to a few hours ahead and then microwave or steam gently to reheat before adding the rest of the flavorings.

1½ cups wild rice, rinsed

1½ tablespoons unsalted butter

⅓ cup thinly sliced scallions (white part only)

3 tablespoons finely grated orange zest

5 tablespoons fresh orange juice; more to taste

¾ cup dried cranberries, coarsely chopped

⅓ cup hazelnuts, lightly toasted on a baking sheet in a 350°F oven and coarsely chopped (skins on or off)

¼ teaspoon kosher salt; more to taste

Freshly ground black pepper

Put the wild rice in a large saucepan and cover with water by about an inch. Bring to a boil. Immediately reduce the heat to low, cover, and simmer until the rice is tender and most of the grains have popped open, 40 to 60 minutes (add a little more water during cooking if the rice is getting too dry; be sure to taste for tenderness). Pour the rice into a colander or sieve to drain well.

In the same saucepan, melt the butter over medium heat. Add the scallions and cook, stirring a few times, until softened, about 2 minutes. Remove from the heat and add the cooked rice, along with the orange zest and juice, cranberries, and hazelnuts; fluff with a fork to blend. Season with the salt and pepper to taste. Serve immediately.

—BETH DOOLEY & LUCIA WATSON

Wheatberries with
FRAGRANT SPICES,
CURRANTS & ALMONDS

Soaking the wheatberries will hasten their cooking time. To get farther ahead, you can even cook them up to three days ahead, drain well, and refrigerate. Add them to the basmati rice and spices just at the end of cooking to warm through.

1 cup wheatberries, soaked for 4 hours or overnight

6 cups water

Table salt

¼ cup olive oil or unsalted butter

1 medium onion, cut into medium dice

8 scallions (white and light green parts only), chopped

½ teaspoon ground allspice

½ teaspoon ground cinnamon; more to taste

1 cup basmati or other long-grain white rice

⅔ cup dried currants or coarsely chopped raisins

1½ cups homemade or low-salt chicken or vegetable broth

⅔ cup (3 ounces) slivered almonds, lightly toasted on a baking sheet in a 350°F oven

¼ cup chopped fresh flat-leaf parsley

2 tablespoons grated lemon zest

Freshly ground black pepper

Drain the wheatberries and then combine them with the water and about 1 teaspoon salt in a medium saucepan. Bring to a boil, then reduce the heat to low, cover, and simmer until tender but pleasantly chewy, 25 to 50 minutes. Drain well.

Meanwhile, heat the oil or butter in a medium saucepan over medium low. Add the onion and scallions; cook until tender and translucent, about 7 minutes. Stir in the allspice, cinnamon, and rice, cook until the spices are fragrant, 1 to 2 minutes, then add the currants or raisins, broth, and salt to taste. Bring to a boil, turn the heat to low, cover, and simmer until the liquid is just absorbed and the rice is tender, 12 to 15 minutes.

In a large serving bowl, combine the wheatberries, rice mixture, and almonds. Stir in the parsley and lemon zest, adjust the salt, pepper, and cinnamon and serve. —JOYCE GOLDSTEIN

Pies
& Tarts

For some, it can't be Thanksgiving without a slice of pumpkin pie. Or was that apple? Or pecan? We give you all the favorites, many with delicious new twists. And we've got advice on making the part of the pie that's the source of anxiety for so many cooks—the pastry. Following our methods, you'll turn out the flakiest, most beautiful pie crusts to showcase whatever filling you choose to make.

CLASSIC
Pie Crust

Rolling the dough between large (24x16-inch) lightly floured sheets of parchment paper reduces the temptation to overflour and makes this easy-handling crust even more user-friendly: Just lift the paper every few passes of the rolling pin to check for sticking and dust with a little flour if needed. If the dough warms up as you work, slide the dough and paper onto a baking sheet and into the refrigerator for 10 minutes. This dough keeps in the freezer for 3 months.

11¼ ounces (2½ cups) all-purpose flour

1 tablespoon granulated sugar

½ teaspoon table salt

½ cup (1 stick) cold unsalted butter, cut into ½-inch pieces

¼ cup cold vegetable shortening, cut into ½-inch pieces

2 teaspoons fresh lemon juice

6 tablespoons ice water

Put the flour, sugar, and salt in a food processor; pulse briefly to combine. Add the butter and shortening; pulse just until coarse crumbs form, about 30 seconds. Add the lemon juice and water. Pulse just until moist crumbs form. Turn the dough onto a work surface and gently shape it into two equal disks 4 or 5 inches in diameter. Wrap in plastic and refrigerate for at least 1 hour or up to 1 day.

FOR A SINGLE-CRUST PIE: Roll one disk of dough between two large pieces of lightly floured parchment into a 14-inch-diameter round that's ⅛ inch thick. Remove the top sheet of parchment. Gently roll the dough around the pin and position the pin over the pie pan. Unroll, gently easing the dough into the pan, gently but firmly pressing the dough against the sides and bottom, taking care not to pull or stretch. With scissors, trim the edge of the dough, leaving a ¾-inch margin from the outer edge of the pan. Tuck this dough under to shape a high-edge crust that rests on top of the rim. Pinch-crimp by pressing toward the center of the pie with the thumb and index finger of one hand and pressing out, right between them, with the index finger of the other hand.

FOR BLIND BAKING: Follow the steps above for making a single-crust pie. Freeze the crust for at least 30 minutes. Heat the oven to 425°F. Line the frozen crust with a large piece of foil, fill with pie weights (or dried beans or raw rice), and bake for 12 minutes. Remove the foil and weights and continue baking the shell until golden, about another 8 minutes, checking for bubbles (push them down gently with the back of a spoon).

FOR A DOUBLE CRUST: Roll out one disk of dough as for a single-crust pie and line a 9-inch pie pan, leaving the excess hanging over the side. Cover loosely with plastic while you roll out the other disk between sheets of parchment. Load the filling into the shell. Brush the

edge of the bottom crust with water. Roll the top crust around the pin and position it over the pie. Gently unroll, centering the dough over the filling. Press the edges together and, with scissors, trim both crusts so they're ½ inch larger than the outer edge of the pie pan. Tuck this dough under to shape a high-edge crust that rests on top of the rim. Pinch-crimp by pressing toward the center of the pie with the thumb and index finger of one hand and pressing out, right between them, with the index finger of the other hand. With a paring knife, slash two or three vent holes in the top crust and bake following the recipe directions.
—ABIGAIL JOHNSON DODGE

TIPS FOR A MORE TENDER PIE CRUST

If your pie crust is tough like cardboard and shrinks drastically during baking, it means that too much gluten formed during mixing and rolling.

When you stir water into flour, proteins in the flour grab the water and one another and form strong, elastic, bubblegum-like sheets of gluten. Gluten is essential in baked goods—it's a big part of what holds them together. Sometimes you need a lot of gluten (for example, when making bread), but for a pie crust, you want just a little, only enough to bind the crust.

For a more tender pie crust, try working the fat (butter, lard, or shortening) into the flour more thoroughly. This greases the proteins, preventing them from forming gluten. The goal is to coat a lot of the flour with the fat for tenderness but to leave some of the flour uncoated, allowing enough gluten to form to hold the crust together. You might also try using more fat and letting it come to room temperature so that it's softer and coats the proteins better. When you add water to the butter-flour mixture, be gentle with the dough to minimize the formation of gluten.

Another way to get a more tender crust is by adding sugar. Flour proteins combine with the sugar instead of the water and other proteins, and very little gluten forms. The high sugar content of cakes and cookies contributes to their tenderness.

Finally, an acidic ingredient such as vinegar can cut tough gluten strands and tenderize crusts, which is why some old-fashioned pie crust recipes call for a small amount of vinegar.

MAKING A LATTICE-TOPPED PIE

Roll out one disk of dough as for a single-crust pie and line a 9-inch pie pan with it, leaving the excess hanging over the sides. Cover loosely with plastic while you roll out the other disk between sheets of parchment into a rectangle that's slightly larger than 14x9 inches. Remove the top sheet of parchment. Trim the dough to an exact 14x9-inch rectangle. Cut 12 strips that are 14 inches long and ¾ inch wide. If the dough gets soft, slide the parchment and dough onto a baking sheet and chill briefly before continuing. On a parchment-lined baking sheet, arrange 6 strips horizontally, setting them ¾ inch apart; these will be the "bottom" strips. Set the rest aside on a separate piece of parchment; these will be the "top" strips. Make the lattice following the photos that follow.

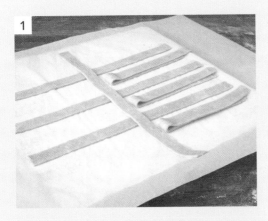

Fold back every other bottom strip, starting closest to you. Slightly right of center, lay one top strip vertically.

Unfold the folded strips and fold back the other three strips. Lay a second top strip ¾ inch to the left of the first.

Unfold the folded strips. Now fold back alternating strips on the right, starting at the top. Lay a strip ¾ inch to the right of the center strip; unfold the folded strips. Repeat left and right with the rest of the strips.

Dab a little water between the strips where they overlap, pressing gently to seal. Cover loosely with plastic and put the baking sheet in the fridge for 20 minutes.

Remove the lattice from the fridge, remove the plastic, and put your palm under the parchment at the center of the lattice. Lift the parchment and invert the lattice onto the filling.

Trim the crust, leaving a ½-inch margin from the edge of the pie pan. Press the edges together, fold them under, crimp or flute the edges, and bake.

BUTTER
Pie Dough
YIELDS 24 OUNCES

This recipe yields 24 ounces, enough for one Apple Pie Covered with Leaves (page 153), or one Pumpkin Pie with a Leafy Rim (page 166).

11¼ ounces (2½ cups) all-purpose flour

¼ cup granulated sugar

½ teaspoon table salt

1 cup (2 sticks) cold unsalted butter, cut into ¼-inch cubes

5 to 6 tablespoons ice water

Whisk the flour, sugar, and salt in the bowl of a stand mixer or a large bowl. In the stand mixer (use the paddle attachment on low speed) or in the bowl by hand with a pastry blender, cut the butter into the flour until the pieces are no bigger than peas. The texture will be floury with flecks of butter; it won't be homogenous. Add 5 tablespoons of the water and mix for a few seconds on low, just long enough to let the dough pull together; if needed, add the remaining 1 tablespoon water. Cut the dough in half, pat each into a ball, and flatten each into a thick disk. Roll out the dough right away, as instructed in the specific recipe.

—CAROLYN WEIL

PRESS-IN
Cookie Crust

YIELDS ONE 9½-INCH CRUST

This shortcut crust with just three ingredients—cookie crumbs, a little sugar, and melted butter—makes a delicious base for stylish holiday tarts. To save even more time, you can use purchased graham cracker crumbs, found in the baking aisle of the supermarket.

1 cup finely ground cookies (ground in a food processor); choose one from the following: about 25 chocolate wafers, 8 whole graham crackers, or 35 vanilla wafers (such as Nabisco® Famous Chocolate Wafers, Honey Maid® Grahams, or Nilla® Vanilla Wafers)

2 tablespoons granulated sugar

3 tablespoons unsalted butter, melted

Position a rack in the middle of the oven and heat the oven to 350°F. Have ready an ungreased 9½-inch fluted tart pan with a removable bottom.

In a medium bowl, mix the cookie crumbs and sugar with a fork until well blended. Drizzle the melted butter over the crumbs and mix with the fork or your fingers until the crumbs are evenly moistened. Put the crumbs in the tart pan and use your hands to spread them so they coat the bottom of the pan and start to climb the sides. Use your fingers to pinch and press some of the crumbs around the inside edge of the pan to cover the sides evenly and create a wall about a scant ¼ inch thick. Redistribute the remaining crumbs evenly over the bottom of the pan and press firmly to make a compact layer. (A metal measuring cup with straight sides and a flat base is ideal for doing this.)

Tip

Lay a piece of plastic wrap over the crumbs as you spread them so they won't stick to your hands.

Bake the crust until it smells nutty and fragrant (crusts made with lighter-colored cookies will brown slightly), about 10 minutes. Set the baked crust in its pan on a rack and let cool. The crust can be made up to one day ahead and stored at room temperature, wrapped well in plastic. —ABIGAIL JOHNSON DODGE

Apple Pie
COVERED WITH LEAVES

Classic apple pie is dressed up with a gorgeous top crust of leafy pastry cutouts arranged in over-lapping concentric circles. Use any tart baking apple you prefer; Braeburn, Empire, Jonathan, Jonagold, and Northern Spy are some of our favorites for this pie. To keep the pastry leaves uniform in size, first make a leaf pattern using parchment, or use a leaf-shaped cookie cutter.

1 recipe Butter Pie Dough (page 150), divided into two disks

5 to 6 firm, tart apples

½ cup granulated sugar

2 tablespoons all-purpose flour

¾ teaspoon ground cinnamon

¼ teaspoon ground nutmeg

⅛ teaspoon table salt

1 to 2 tablespoons unsalted butter, cut up

On a lightly floured work surface, roll one of the dough disks into a 12-inch round that's ⅛ inch thick (trim an edge to check the thickness). Fold the dough in half, ease it into a 9-inch pie pan, and unfold it. Press the dough up the sides and over the rim of the pan and trim it to the outer edge. Chill the dough while you cut out the leaves.

Pat the scraps into the bottom of the second disk and roll out the dough to ⅛ inch thick (the shape doesn't matter). Using a paring knife or a leaf-shaped cookie cutter, cut out as many 2x1½-inch leaves as you can. Use the dull edge of a paring knife, pressing just less than halfway through the dough, to indent each leaf with thin lines like leaf veins. Pat the scraps together, roll out the dough again, and cut out more leaves. You'll need 45 to 55 leaves to cover the pie. (You can make smaller or larger leaves, if you like; you'll need more or fewer leaves accordingly.) Set the leaves aside in a cool place (but not in the refrigerator).

Peel, quarter, and core the apples. Cut them into ¼-inch-thick slices to get 7 cups. Put the apples in a large bowl and sprinkle with the sugar, flour, cinnamon, nutmeg, and salt. Toss gently and layer the apples into *(continued)*

Tip

To make the leafy top crust, casually overlap the leaves in concentric circles toward the middle of the pie. Try not to have too much overlapping, because the double-thick areas will take longer to bake through.

the pie shell, tucking in any apples to create an even, smooth dome. Dot the apples with large flecks of the butter.

Starting at the rim of the pan, stick the dough leaves on the crust and apples, using a little water on the bottom of the leaves to help them adhere. You needn't press the leaves together; they'll seal during baking. Continue to overlap the leaves in concentric circles toward the middle of the pie, minimizing the overlapping areas, until the apples are completely covered.

Chill the pie in the refrigerator for 15 minutes. Meanwhile, position two racks in the lower third of the oven, set a foil-lined baking sheet on the lowest rack (to catch any drippings from the pie), and heat the oven to 350°F.

Bake the pie on the second-lowest rack until the crust is deep golden all over and the apples are tender when pierced with a long, thin knife blade, 60 to 80 minutes. Let the pie cool completely before serving so the juices set up and the filling won't be runny. Serve at room temperature or warm briefly in a 400°F oven. —CAROLYN WEIL

GETTING AHEAD WITH A FANCY PIE

If you spread out the preparations, making this gorgeous pie isn't any more work than making a simple dessert. Here's how: Make the dough, roll it out right away, and lay it in a freezerproof pie or tart pan. Seal the pan in a plastic bag and freeze. Make the leaf cutouts and freeze them on a baking sheet. When they're hard, put them in a freezer container. The crust and leaves will hold for up to a month in the freezer. To thaw the apple pie shell and leaves, let them sit at room temperature (leaves in a single layer) until they're pliable. Then assemble the pie following the directions.

MAKING A PERFECT PILE OF PASTRY LEAVES

Cut out as many leaves as you can with a paring knife. You can also use a leaf-shaped cookie cutter.

Vein the leaves with the dull side of the knife. Use gentle but steady pressure to indent each leaf, pressing just less than halfway through the dough.

Press the leaves on the rim of the empty pie shell, overlapping each one slightly and using a little water on the bottom of the leaves to stick them together. Let the widest part of each leaf protrude slightly from the edge of the crust.

APPLE CIDER *Pie*

YIELDS ONE 9-INCH PIE; SERVES 8

A sprinkling of crushed sugar cubes baked onto the top crust adds sparkle and sweetness.

FOR THE FILLING:

3 pounds Golden Delicious or Gala apples, peeled, cored, cut into ¾-inch-thick slices, and then halved crosswise

⅔ cup apple cider

½ to ⅔ cup packed light brown sugar, to taste

1 teaspoon ground cinnamon

¼ teaspoon ground nutmeg

3 tablespoons cornstarch

FOR THE DOUBLE CRUST:

1 recipe Classic Pie Crust (page 146)

3 tablespoons heavy cream

¼ cup sugar cubes (about 12 small), coarsely crushed

In a large nonreactive pot, mix the apples, all but 2 tablespoons of the cider, the brown sugar, cinnamon, and nutmeg. Bring to a boil, stirring often, until the sugar has dissolved and the apples are evenly coated. In a small bowl, mix the cornstarch and remaining 2 tablespoons cider into a paste; add this to the apples. Stirring constantly, boil until the liquid is thickened and clear, about 1 minute (you're not cooking the apples, just thickening the juices). Taste and adjust the spices if needed. Remove from the heat and let cool.

Position racks in the lower third and middle of the oven. Set a foil-lined baking sheet on the lower rack to catch drips and heat the oven to 425°F. Fit the bottom crust into a 9-inch pie pan, add the filling, and finish with the top crust as directed on page 146. Brush the heavy cream over the top crust and sprinkle with the crushed sugar cubes, pressing lightly to secure the chunks. Cut at least three vent holes. Bake on the middle rack until the crust is golden and the apples are tender when pierced with a knife, about 55 minutes. If the top starts browning too quickly, tent the pie with foil. —ABIGAIL JOHNSON DODGE

PEAR-RAISIN *Pie*

YIELDS ONE 9-INCH PIE; SERVES 8 TO 10

Pears are one of the few fruits that don't ripen on the tree, so most likely they'll be underripe at the market. To speed up ripening, place them in a paper bag on the counter and check them daily; they're ready to use when they yield to gentle pressure near the stem. (Don't wait until pears are soft in the middle; at that point they're probably overripe.) Keep ripe pears in the coldest part of the fridge. If you don't have any bourbon on hand, use brandy or skip the alcohol altogether.

FOR THE FILLING:

3 pounds firm, ripe pears (like Bartletts), peeled, cored, cut into ¾-inch-thick slices, then halved

¾ cup raisins

⅔ cup packed dark or light brown sugar

1 teaspoon grated lemon zest

2 teaspoons fresh lemon juice

½ teaspoon ground cinnamon

¼ teaspoon ground cloves

Pinch ground mace

Pinch table salt

½ cup bourbon

3 tablespoons cornstarch

FOR THE LATTICE CRUST:

1 recipe Classic Pie Crust (page 146)

2 tablespoons milk

3 tablespoons finely chopped walnuts mixed with 1 tablespoon granulated sugar

Position racks in the bottom and middle of the oven and set a foil-lined baking sheet on the lower rack to catch any drips. Heat the oven to 425°F.

In a large saucepan, combine the pears, raisins, brown sugar, lemon zest, juice, spices, salt, and all but 2 tablespoons of the bourbon. Cook over medium-high heat, stirring gently, until the sugar is dissolved and the pears begin to release some liquid, about 4 minutes. Mix the cornstarch with the remaining 2 tablespoons bourbon; add this to the pears. Bring to a boil, stirring frequently, and cook until the liquid is clear, about 1 minute. Let the filling cool to room temperature.

Meanwhile, roll out one disk of the dough and line a 9-inch pie pan. Trim the excess to ¾ inch from the pan's outer edge. Cover with plastic wrap and set aside. Roll out the other disk and assemble the lattice as directed on page 148. Remove the plastic from the bottom shell and fill it with the cooled pear mixture. Transfer the lattice to the pie, sealing as described. Brush the lattice with the milk and sprinkle the nut-and-sugar mixture over the pie. Bake until the pears are just tender when pierced with a knife, 50 to 55 minutes. If the lattice browns too quickly, tent the pie with foil. —ABIGAIL JOHNSON DODGE

GINGER CRANBERRY-PEAR
Tartlets

YIELDS 12 TARTLETS

Crystallized ginger (sold at specialty foods stores and in the spice or dried fruit section of some supermarkets) accents this filling with sweet pears and tart cranberries. You can fill and bake these and the Pecan Tartlets (page 162) and Pumpkin Tartlets (page 163) up to four weeks ahead and freeze them: Put the baked and cooled tartlets on a shallow pan and freeze until firm, then layer them between waxed paper in an airtight container. They will also hold for three days in the fridge (covered with waxed paper and foil—not plastic wrap). To refresh the tartlets, bake, uncovered, at 325°F until warm, 5 to 7 minutes if refrigerated, 12 to 15 minutes if frozen.

1 cup fresh cranberries, picked over and rinsed

⅓ cup granulated sugar

⅓ cup orange juice

2 medium, slightly underripe pears (like Anjou), about ¾ pound total, peeled, cored, and cut into ½-inch chunks

⅓ cup golden raisins

4 teaspoons minced crystallized ginger

A few drops pure vanilla extract

12 muffin cups lined with Sweet Tartlet Dough (page 160)

In a 3-quart saucepan, cook the cranberries, sugar, and orange juice over medium heat just until the berries begin to pop. Reduce the heat to a simmer, partially cover, and cook for 5 minutes. Add the pears, raisins, and ginger. Cook over low heat with the lid ajar until the pears are translucent, stirring gently if necessary, 10 to 12 minutes. Uncover and continue cooking until the liquid is syrupy and has reduced to about 2 tablespoons, about 2 minutes. Remove from the heat and gently stir in the vanilla (avoid crushing the pears). Let cool to room temperature; the mixture thickens as it stands.

Position a rack in the lower third of the oven. Heat the oven to 375°F.

Spoon the filling into the dough-lined muffin cups. Bake until the pastry is golden brown and the fruit is bubbling, about 30 minutes. Let cool for 10 minutes. Run a thin knife around the tartlets to loosen and then let them cool until they're firm enough to handle, about another 15 minutes. Using the tip of a small knife, gently lift the tartlets from the pan and set them on a wire rack to cool completely. —CAROLE WALTER

Ginger-Cranberry
Pear Tartlets, Pecan
Tartlets (page 162),
and Pumpkin Tartlets
(page 163).

= ꙮ =

SWEET TARTLET DOUGH

This buttery crust is easy to handle, and can be made ahead and frozen for up to one month. The baking will go faster if you use three standard medium-size muffin tins (each cup measuring 2¾ inches), but if you don't have three, simply bake the tartlets in batches. A tartlet tamper (sold at cookware stores) is the ideal tool for pressing dough balls into muffin cups, but your fingers or a small glass will work, too. If you can't find superfine sugar, make your own by processing granulated sugar in a food processor for a few seconds.

10⅛ ounces (2¼ cups) all-purpose flour	1 large egg
⅓ cup superfine sugar	1 large egg yolk
¼ teaspoon table salt	1 tablespoon ice water
1 cup (2 sticks) cold, unsalted butter, cut into ½-inch cubes	¾ teaspoon vanilla extract

YIELDS 3 DOZEN 2-INCH TARTLET SHELLS

Put the flour, sugar, and salt in a food processor; pulse 3 to 4 times to blend. Distribute the butter in the bowl and pulse 7 to 8 times, then process until the mixture resembles coarse meal, 8 to 10 seconds. In a small bowl, beat the whole egg, egg yolk, water, and vanilla with a fork. Pour the egg mixture over the flour mixture, pulse 5 to 6 times, and then process until the mixture just begins to form a mass, 8 to 10 seconds. Empty the dough onto a lightly floured work surface and knead 6 to 8 times, until the dough is just smooth and malleable. Shape it into an evenly thick 6-inch square. Using a bench knife or the dull side of a long knife, score the dough at 1-inch intervals so you get thirty-six 1-inch squares. Cover the dough with plastic wrap and chill for at least 20 minutes.

Lightly spray the muffin tins with vegetable oil (not necessary for nonstick tins). Using the score lines as a guide, cut the dough into thirty-six 1-inch pieces. Roll each piece into a ball between your palms (lightly flour your hands, if necessary). Put 1 ball in the center of each muffin cup. If you have a wooden tart tamper, flour it lightly. Press the wider end onto a ball of dough until it thins out and begins coming up the sides of the cup, and then twist the tamper slightly to release it. Use the tamper's narrower end to push the dough halfway up the sides and to smooth out the dough where the sides meet the bottom.

If you don't have a tart tamper, use a narrow, flat-bottomed glass or your fingers, lightly floured, to press the dough into the cups.

Tilt the muffin tin to see if the dough reaches the same level in all the cups; also check for any holes in the dough (this could cause the tartlet to stick to the pan). Rub your thumb around the rim of the dough in each cup for a clean, smooth edge. Slightly less than ½ inch of each cup should be exposed. Chill for at least 10 minutes to firm the dough before filling it.

MINIATURE TARTS NEEDN'T BE FUSSY

Don't bother fluting the edges, but do smooth the rim by running your thumb along the dough's top edge.

A lightly floured tartlet tamper is the ideal tool for pressing dough balls into muffin cups, but your fingers or a small glass will work, too.

PECAN
Tartlets | YIELDS 12 TARTLETS

This petite portion of pecan pie is satisfyingly sweet but not too gooey. It's simply crunchy toasted pecans sprinkled over a mouthwatering brown sugar filling. And you can bake and freeze the tartlets up to one month ahead of time. To serve, simply pop them in the oven until warm. (For detailed make-and-freeze directions, see the Gingery Cranberry-Pear Tartlets on page 158.)

2 large eggs, lightly beaten

1 tablespoon heavy cream

¼ cup packed light brown sugar

1 teaspoon all-purpose flour

Pinch table salt

½ cup light corn syrup

1 tablespoon unsalted butter, melted

¾ teaspoon pure vanilla extract

12 muffin cups lined with Sweet Tartlet Dough (page 160)

1 cup (4 ounces) broken pecans, lightly toasted on a baking sheet in a 350°F oven

Position a rack to the lower third of the oven. Heat the oven to 375°F.

In a medium bowl, blend the eggs and cream. In another bowl, combine the brown sugar, flour, and salt. Stir the dry ingredients into the egg mixture, along with the corn syrup and melted butter; don't overmix. Stir in the vanilla. Transfer the filling to a measuring cup with a spout and pour into the dough-lined muffin cups. Sprinkle the pecans evenly over the tops. Bake until the pastry is golden brown, 28 to 30 minutes. Let cool for 10 minutes. Run a thin knife around the tartlets to loosen and then let them cool until they're firm enough to handle, about another 15 minutes. Using the tip of a small knife, gently lift the tartlets from the pan and set them on a wire rack to cool completely. —CAROLE WALTER

PUMPKIN *Tartlets* | YIELDS 12 TARTLETS

These neat little mini tartlets are made to order for guests who are full but simply can't pass on pumpkin pie. Three of these dainty tarts make a serving: offer three-of-a-kind or a trio of different tartlets—Pumpkin, Pecan (page 162), and Gingery Cranberry-Pear (page 158)—on each plate. A dollop of whipped cream and a very thin strip of orange zest, twisted into a knot, makes a lovely garnish. For make-and-freeze directions, see the Gingery Cranberry-Pear Tartlets on page 158.

1 large egg yolk

⅔ cup canned pure solid-pack pumpkin (not pumpkin pie filling)

⅓ cup heavy cream

¼ cup packed light brown sugar

½ teaspoon grated orange zest

½ teaspoon ground cinnamon

⅛ teaspoon ground nutmeg

⅛ teaspoon table salt

A few dashes ground cloves

12 muffin cups lined with Sweet Tartlet Dough (page 160)

Position a rack to the lower third of the oven. Heat the oven to 375°F.

Put all the ingredients, except the dough, in a food processor and pulse just until smooth, 5 to 6 times; don't overprocess. Empty the filling into a measuring cup with a spout and

pour into the dough-lined muffin cups. Bake until the pastry is golden brown, 30 to 35 minutes. Let cool for 10 minutes. Run a thin knife around the tartlets to loosen and then let them cool until they're firm enough to handle, about another 15 minutes. Using the tip of a small knife, gently lift the tartlets from the pan and set them on a wire rack to cool completely. —CAROLE WALTER

PUMPKIN, SWEET POTATO & COCONUT *Pie*

YIELDS ONE 9-INCH PIE; SERVES 8

Puréed sweet potato absorbs some of the moisture in the canned pumpkin, resulting in a more lus-cious filling. Coconut milk adds richness and just a subtle hint of coconut flavor. In fact, this pie is so delicious that you might want to make two at a time. If you do, use three whole eggs when doubling the filling. The sweet potatoes can be puréed, then chilled or frozen well before you assemble the pie. Look for canned Thai coconut milk in the Asian foods section of the supermarket.

1¼ pounds sweet potatoes, peeled and cut into 1-inch chunks

1 small cinnamon stick, broken into pieces

3 whole cloves

1 small star anise, crumbled

One 1-inch piece fresh ginger, peeled and cut into ¼-inch-thick slices

One 15-ounce can pure solid-pack pumpkin (not pumpkin pie filling)

1 large egg, lightly beaten

1 large egg yolk, lightly beaten

2 tablespoons unsalted butter, melted and cooled

½ cup granulated sugar

½ cup packed light brown sugar

2 tablespoons all-purpose flour

¾ teaspoon table salt

½ cup well-stirred canned coconut milk (not coconut cream)

½ recipe Classic Pie Crust (page 146), rolled out, fitted into a 9-inch pie plate, edge trimmed, and chilled

¾ cup cold whipping cream, whipped to soft peaks with 1½ tablespoons granulated sugar

In a medium saucepan, combine the sweet potatoes, cinnamon stick pieces, cloves, star anise, and ginger slices with enough water to just cover the contents. Bring to a boil, reduce the heat, and simmer, uncovered, until the sweet potatoes are very tender when pierced with a fork or skewer, about 10 minutes. Drain the potatoes, reserving the cooking liquid. Return the potatoes to the pot over low heat and toss to dry them a bit. Discard the cinnamon, cloves, and star anise.

Force the warm potatoes through a ricer, a food mill, or a sieve. Boil the liquid, if needed, until reduced to ¼ cup. Let the sweet potato mash and the liquid cool. (The sweet potatoes and spiced liquid can be prepared up to three days ahead and refrigerated. Bring each to room temperature before proceeding with the recipe. Each of these elements can also be frozen for up to three months; thaw overnight in the refrigerator before bringing to room temperature.)

Position a rack in the lower half of the oven; heat the oven to 350°F.

In a large bowl, whisk the pumpkin with the sweet potato purée. Whisk in the whole egg, egg yolk, melted butter, and reserved spiced liquid. In a separate bowl, stir the granulated and brown sugars with a wire whisk until any large lumps of brown sugar are gone. Sift the flour and salt over the sugars; stir to blend. Add this to the pumpkin mixture and stir well until no pockets of sugar are visible. Blend in the coconut milk.

Scrape the filling into the chilled pie shell; smooth the top. Bake for 1¾ to 2 hours, turning the pie several times so it bakes evenly. The point of a thin-bladed knife should come out clean when inserted into the center of the filling, and the edges of the surface will be unevenly cracked. If the edges of the pastry darken too much before the filling is cooked, cover them with a pie shield or strips of foil. Transfer the pie to a wire rack and let cool completely before serving with mounds of the lightly sweetened whipped cream. —REGAN DALEY

Tip

To pinch-crimp an edge, press out with the thumb and index finger of one hand and press toward the center of the pie, right between them, with the index finger of the other hand.

—ABIGAIL JOHNSON DODGE

Pumpkin Pie
WITH A LEAFY RIM

YIELDS ONE 9-INCH PIE; SERVES 8

Pumpkin pie, which often looks so humble, gets a pretty leafy rim instead of a fluted one, and a starburst of eight sugar-sprinkled pastry leaves on top for a professional look. Metal and unglazed ceramic pie pans work better than glass for this pie because the crust doesn't shrink as much during the blind baking. Unglazed ceramic has the added advantage of making the crust extra crisp. You can double this recipe, using one 15-ounce can of pumpkin; it will be just shy of 2 cups, but that's fine. Serve this with freshly whipped cream, if you like.

1 recipe Butter Pie Dough (page 150), divided into two disks	¾ teaspoon ground cinnamon
Granulated sugar for sprinkling	½ teaspoon ground ginger
2 large eggs	¼ teaspoon ground cloves
1 large egg yolk	¼ teaspoon ground nutmeg
½ cup packed light brown sugar	½ cup dark corn syrup
¼ teaspoon table salt	1 cup canned pure solid-pack pumpkin (not pumpkin pie filling)
	1½ cups heavy cream

On a lightly floured work surface, roll one of the dough disks into a rough round that's 12 inches in diameter and ⅛ inch thick (trim an edge to check thickness). Fold the dough in half and ease it into a 9-inch pie pan (preferably metal or unglazed ceramic), then unfold it. If using a metal or ceramic pan, trim the dough to the edge of the pan. If using a glass pan, trim the dough to ⅛ inch of the edge of the pan (the overhang compensates for shrinkage). Cover with plastic wrap and refrigerate.

Press the scraps together and roll them out again. Using a paring knife, cut out at least 32 small leaves just slightly larger than 2 inches long and ½ inch wide. (For uniform leaves, you can make a leaf pattern with parchment or use a leaf-shaped cookie cutter.) Use the dull edge of a paring knife, pressing just less than halfway through the dough, to indent each leaf with thin lines like leaf veins. If you need more dough, borrow a large pinch from the second disk of dough (save the rest of the second dough disk for another pie).

Put eight of the prettiest leaves on a parchment-lined baking sheet. Sprinkle with a pinch of granulated sugar to add a little sparkle and refrigerate. Press the remaining small leaves on the rim of the pie shell, overlapping each one slightly and using a little water on the bottom of the leaves to stick them together. Let the widest part of each leaf protrude slightly from the edge of the crust. Chill the crust well, about 1 hour in the refrigerator.

At least 20 minutes before you're ready to bake the crust, position a rack in the middle of the oven and heat the oven to 350°F.

Cover the crust with foil, gently folding the foil completely over the leaf edge. Cover the bottom with a generous amount of pie weights or dried beans. Bake until the crust is pale and no longer looks wet and the sides are golden, 30 to 35 minutes. Remove the foil and weights or beans and prick the crust very lightly with a fork (but don't pierce through it). Continue to bake until the crust is golden all over, another 5 to 10 minutes. Make a foil ring that covers the rim of the crust and set aside.

In a large bowl, whisk the whole eggs, egg yolk, and brown sugar. Add the salt and spices and mix well. Add the corn syrup and pumpkin and whisk until smooth. Stir in the cream. Pour the filling into crust and carefully set the foil ring on top. Handle the pie plate gently when you put it in (and take it out of) the oven; the leafy rim is fragile. Bake until the custard is risen around the edges and is still jiggly (but no longer wavy) in the center, 40 to 50 minutes. Let cool on a wire rack; the custard will set up more as it cools.

Bake the eight reserved small leaves until golden, 8 to 10 minutes. Let cool and set aside. Let the pie cool to room temperature, then chill for at least 2 hours.

To serve, set the baked leaves on the surface of the pie in a starburst pattern. Warm in a 375°F oven for a few minutes to take the chill off the crust. —CAROLYN WEIL

Bourbon Pumpkin Tart
WITH WALNUT STREUSEL

This is the ideal make-ahead or bring-along dessert: The baked tart can be chilled overnight, and it's delicious served slightly chilled, at room temperature, or warm. If baking it one day ahead, be sure to let the tart cool completely before wrapping it in plastic. The pastry dough will keep for up to one week in the fridge or for up to a month in the freezer.

FOR THE CRUST:

9 ounces (2 cups) all-purpose flour

⅓ cup granulated sugar

1 teaspoon finely grated orange zest

½ teaspoon table salt

11 tablespoons cold unsalted butter, cut into ½-inch cubes

1 large egg, lightly beaten

¼ cup heavy cream; more if needed

FOR THE FILLING:

One 15-ounce can pure solid-pack pumpkin (not pumpkin pie filling)

3 large eggs

½ cup granulated sugar

¼ cup packed dark brown sugar

2 tablespoons unbleached all-purpose flour

1 teaspoon ground ginger

1 teaspoon ground cinnamon

¼ teaspoon ground cloves

¼ teaspoon table salt

½ cup heavy cream

¼ cup bourbon

FOR THE STREUSEL:

3½ ounces (¾ cup) all-purpose flour

⅓ cup granulated sugar

⅓ cup packed dark brown sugar

½ teaspoon ground cinnamon

½ teaspoon table salt

½ cup (1 stick) cold unsalted butter, cut into ½-inch cubes

¾ cup walnut halves, lightly toasted on a baking sheet in a 350°F oven, then coarsely chopped

¼ cup chopped crystallized ginger

Lightly sweetened whipped cream for garnish (optional)

MAKE THE CRUST: Whisk the flour, sugar, orange zest, and salt in the bowl of a stand mixer or a mixing bowl. In the stand mixer (use the paddle attachment on low speed) or in the bowl by hand with a pastry blender, cut the butter into the flour until the mixture looks crumbly, with pieces of butter about the size of dried peas. Add the egg and cream, mixing on low speed until the dough is just combined. If the dough is too dry to come together, add more cream, 1 tablespoon at a time. Gently mold the dough into a 1-inch-thick disk and wrap in plastic. Refrigerate for at least 1 hour or for up to a week; the dough can also be frozen for up to a month (defrost overnight in the refrigerator).

MAKE THE FILLING: Spoon the pumpkin into a large bowl. Whisk in the eggs, one at a time, until thoroughly incorporated. Add both sugars, the flour, ginger, cinnamon, cloves, and salt. Whisk for about 30 seconds. Whisk in the heavy cream and bourbon.

MAKE THE STREUSEL TOPPING: Combine the flour, both sugars, cinnamon, and salt in a food processor fitted with a metal blade. Pulse briefly to mix. Add the butter and pulse until blended into the dry ingredients and the mixture is crumbly. Remove the blade and stir in the walnuts and crystallized ginger.

ASSEMBLE AND BAKE: Position a rack in the middle of the oven and heat the oven to 350°F. Take the tart dough from the refrigerator and let it warm up until pliable, 5 to 15 minutes. Unwrap the dough and set it on a lightly floured work surface. With as few passes of the rolling pin as possible, roll the disk into a 13-inch round about ³⁄₁₆ inch thick. Drape the round into an 11-inch fluted tart pan with a removable bottom, gently fitting it into the contours of the pan. Fold the excess dough into the sides of the pan and press to create an edge that's flush with the top of the pan and about ½ inch thick.

Pour the filling into the crust. Scatter the streusel topping evenly over the filling. Bake until the topping is evenly cooked and it no longer looks wet in the center, 50 to 65 minutes. Let the tart cool on a wire rack for at least 2 hours before serving (or, once it has completely cooled, wrap it in plastic and refrigerate overnight; before serving, let it sit at room temperature for 1 to 2 hours). Serve warm, at room temperature, or slightly chilled, with whipped cream, if you like.

—REBECCA RATHER

CHOCOLATE
Pecan Pie

YIELDS ONE 9-INCH PIE; SERVES 8 TO 10

For extra sheen, brush the top of this pie with a little pure maple syrup just before serving.

2 tablespoons cold unsalted butter, cut into chunks

2 ounces unsweetened chocolate, finely chopped

1¼ cups light corn syrup

¾ cup pure maple syrup

3 large eggs

1 tablespoon Kahlùa or other coffee-flavored liqueur

½ recipe Classic Pie Crust (page 146), rolled out, fitted into a 9-inch pie plate, and blind baked

1½ cups (6 ounces) pecan halves, lightly toasted on a baking sheet in a 350°F oven

Position a rack in the middle of the oven and heat the oven to 350°F.

In a large saucepan, combine the butter, chocolate, corn syrup, and maple syrup over medium-high heat and bring to a boil, whisking frequently. The mixture will bubble vigorously once it starts to boil. Continue whisking and cooking until the mixture emulsifies, about 5 minutes. Let cool, then whisk in the eggs one at a time, then the Kahlùa. Pour the filling into the baked pie shell. Arrange the pecan halves randomly on top of the filling. Bake until the filling's edges are puffed and the center jiggles like gelatin when you nudge the pan, 40 to 45 minutes. Let cool on a wire rack and serve at room temperature. —ABIGAIL JOHNSON DODGE

HOW TO PREVENT SHRINKING PIE CRUSTS

In our time in the test kitchen, we've found that sometimes pie crusts shrink during blind baking and sometimes they don't. We conducted several rounds of tests, changing variables like the type of pan, oven temperature, and chilling time. We've discovered that crusts are less apt to shrink in metal and unglazed ceramic pie pans and shrink most dramatically in Pyrex pans, slipping off the rim and down the sides of the smooth glass.

Chilling time doesn't seem to make a big difference, but oven temperature does. Higher baking temperatures (425°F) encourage shrinkage, while lower heat (350°F) minimizes it. Food scientist Shirley O. Corriher explains: "At higher temperatures, the gluten proteins in the flour tighten up. If they're heated more gently, they shrink less." Other factors that can cause shrinkage are overhandling the dough and not chilling the dough sufficiently before baking. To avoid shrinking crusts, use a metal or unglazed ceramic pie plate and blind bake the dough at 350°F. If you only have a glass pie plate, you can still blind bake your crust. Just be sure to trim the dough a tad beyond the rim of the pan, perhaps ⅛ inch. This slight overhang will help compensate for the shrinkage and slippage. But don't go overboard: Too much overhang can cause the crust to crack during baking.

Chocolate Truffle Tart
WITH WHIPPED VANILLA MASCARPONE TOPPING

YIELDS ONE 9½-INCH TART;
SERVES 12 TO 16

Think of this refreshing icebox dessert as a sophisticated no-bake pudding pie. It's all about the chocolate, so use the best you can afford. Mascarpone is a soft, fresh Italian cheese, similar to ricotta but made with cream instead of milk. (It's one of the key ingredients in tiramisù.) The best source for mascarpone is a good Italian market, but it's also available at many supermarkets.

FOR THE FILLING:

12 ounces bittersweet chocolate, finely chopped (see How to Chop Chocolate, page 194)

¼ cup (½ stick) unsalted butter, cut into tablespoons

1 cup whole milk

1 teaspoon pure vanilla extract

¼ teaspoon table salt

1 recipe Press-In Cookie Crust (page 151) made with graham crackers, baked and cooled

FOR THE TOPPING:

½ pound mascarpone cheese, at room temperature

¾ cup heavy cream

¼ cup granulated sugar

½ teaspoon pure vanilla extract

MAKE THE FILLING: Melt the chocolate and butter with the milk in a medium bowl in a microwave or in the top of a double boiler over medium heat. Add the vanilla and salt; whisk until well blended and smooth. Set aside, whisking occasionally, until room temperature and slightly thickened, about 1 hour. (For faster cooling, refrigerate the filling until thickened to a pudding consistency, about 30 minutes, whisking and scraping the sides of the bowl with a rubber spatula every 5 minutes.)

With a spatula, scrape the filling into the crust and spread evenly, taking care not to disturb the edge of the crust. Let cool completely, cover with plastic, and refrigerate until the filling is set, about 4 hours and up to 8 hours before proceeding with the recipe.

Tip

To remove a tart from the pan, set the pan on a wide can and let the outside ring fall away. If it's stubborn, grip the ring with your fingers to coax it off. Slide a long, thin metal spatula between the pan base and the crust and ease the tart onto a flat serving plate.

MAKE THE TOPPING: In a medium bowl, combine the topping ingredients. Using an electric mixer, beat on low speed until almost smooth, 30 to 60 seconds. Increase the speed to medium high and beat until the mixture is thick and holds firm peaks, another 30 to 60 seconds. Don't overbeat. With a rubber or metal spatula, spread the topping over the filling, leaving lots of swirls and peaks. Serve the tart right away or cover loosely and refrigerate, in the pan, for up to 4 hours. Remove the tart from the pan, following the tip at left. —ABIGAIL JOHNSON DODGE

TRIPLE CHOCOLATE
Ice Cream Pie

YIELDS ONE 9-INCH PIE; SERVES 8 TO 12

This pie features a chocolate crust, chocolate ice cream, and chocolate sauce, with a few scoops of coffee and vanilla ice cream added for contrast. You can make it up to two weeks ahead (details in the recipe), which means all that's left to do on Thanksgiving is pull it out of the freezer and serve. The hot fudge sauce will also keep for two weeks in the fridge and months in the freezer, so you might want to make a double batch to have on hand for the next round of winter holidays.

6 ounces (about 30) chocolate wafer cookies

5 tablespoons unsalted butter, melted; more for greasing the pan

2 pints chocolate ice cream, slightly softened

Quick Hot Fudge Sauce (page 175), at room temperature

1 pint coffee ice cream, slightly softened

1 pint vanilla ice cream, slightly softened

Position a rack in the middle of the oven and heat the oven to 350°F. Butter a 9-inch Pyrex or metal pie plate.

Put the cookies in a zip-top plastic bag and crush them with a rolling pin (or process in a food processor) until you have fine crumbs. Measure 1½ cups of crumbs (crush more cookies, if necessary) and put them in a medium bowl. Add the melted butter and stir until the crumbs are evenly moistened. Transfer to the pie plate and, using your fingers, press the mixture evenly into the bottom and up the sides (but not on the rim). Bake for 10 minutes. Let cool completely on a wire rack.

Scoop 1 pint of the chocolate ice cream into the cooled crust and spread it evenly with a rubber spatula. Place in the freezer to firm up for about 30 minutes. Remove the pie from the freezer and, working quickly, drizzle ½ cup of the room-temperature fudge sauce over the ice cream. Using a small ice cream scoop (1½-inch-diameter), scoop round balls of the remaining chocolate and the coffee and vanilla ice creams and arrange them over the fudge sauce layer (you may not need all of the ice cream). Drizzle with about ¼ cup of the remaining fudge sauce, using a squirt bottle if you have one. Freeze until the ice cream is firm, about 2 hours. If not serving right away, loosely cover the pie with waxed paper, then wrap with foil. Freeze for up to two weeks.

To serve, let the pie soften in the refrigerator for 15 to 30 minutes (premium ice cream brands need more time to soften). Meanwhile, gently reheat the remaining fudge sauce in a small saucepan over medium-low heat. Pry the pie out of the pan with a thin metal spatula. (If the pie doesn't pop out, set the pan in a shallow amount of hot water for a minute or two to help the crust release.) Set the pie on a board, cut into wedges, and serve drizzled with more hot fudge sauce, if you like. —LORI LONGBOTHAM

QUICK HOT FUDGE SAUCE

This sauce will keep for at least two weeks in the refrigerator and for several months in the freezer.

1 cup heavy cream

2 tablespoons light corn syrup

Pinch table salt

8 ounces bittersweet chocolate, finely chopped (about 1⅓ cups; see How to Chop Chocolate, page 194)

YIELDS 1½ CUPS

Bring the cream, corn syrup, and salt just to a boil in a medium, heavy-based saucepan over medium-high heat, whisking until combined. Remove the pan from the heat, add the chocolate, and whisk until smooth. Let cool to a bit warmer than room temperature before using in the ice cream pie. The sauce thickens as it cools; you want it warm enough to drizzle but not so warm that it melts the ice cream.

TRIPLE CHOCOLATE
Cheesecake

YIELDS ONE 9-INCH CAKE; SERVES 16

This dense, luxurious cheesecake gets its chocolate power from three sources—the chocolate cookie crust, and both cocoa powder and chocolate in the cheese filling. Take care not to overbeat the filling or you'll end up with a puffed, cracked cake. For best results, have the cream cheese at about 70°F before you start and, if you have a stand mixer, use the paddle attachment instead of regular beaters.

FOR THE CRUST:

1½ cups very finely crushed chocolate cookie crumbs (about 30 Nabisco Famous Chocolate Wafers)

3 tablespoons granulated sugar

⅛ teaspoon ground cinnamon (optional)

¼ cup (½ stick) unsalted butter, melted

FOR THE FILLING:

½ cup sour cream

2 teaspoons pure vanilla extract

1 teaspoon instant coffee granules or instant espresso powder

8 ounces bittersweet chocolate, finely chopped (see How to Chop Chocolate, page 194)

Three 8-ounce packages cream cheese, at room temperature

3 tablespoons natural unsweetened cocoa powder, sifted if lumpy

¼ teaspoon table salt

1¼ cups granulated sugar

3 large eggs, at room temperature

Heat the oven to 400°F. In a medium bowl, stir the cookie crumbs, sugar, and cinnamon (if using) until blended. Drizzle with the melted butter and mix until well blended and the crumbs are evenly moist. Dump the mixture into a 9-inch springform pan and press evenly onto the bottom and about 1 inch up the sides of the pan (to press, use plastic wrap, a straight-sided, flat-based coffee mug, or a tart tamper). Bake for 10 minutes and set on a wire rack to cool. Reduce the oven temperature to 300°F.

In a small bowl, mix the sour cream, vanilla, and coffee granules. Set aside and stir occasionally until the coffee dissolves.

Melt the chocolate in a double boiler over medium heat. Stir until smooth. Set aside to cool slightly.

In a stand mixer fitted with the paddle attachment (or in a large bowl with a hand mixer), beat the cream cheese, cocoa powder, and salt until very smooth and fluffy, scraping the bowl and beaters frequently (and with each subsequent addition). Add the sugar and continue beating until well blended and smooth. Scrape the cooled chocolate into the bowl; beat until blended. Beat in the sour cream mixture until well blended. Add the eggs, one at a time, and beat until just blended. (Don't overbeat the filling once the eggs have been added or the cheesecake will puff too much.) *(continued)*

Pour the filling over the cooled crust, spread evenly, and smooth the top. Bake until the center barely jiggles when nudged, 50 to 60 minutes. The cake will be slightly puffed, with a few little cracks around the edge. Let cool to room temperature on a wire rack and then refrigerate until well chilled, at least a few hours, or overnight for the best texture and flavor. (This cake freezes well, too. Put the unmolded cake in the freezer, uncovered, until the top is cold and firm, then wrap it in two layers of plastic and one layer of foil.)

To remove the cake from the springform and make clean slices, see the instructions on page 183. —ABIGAIL JOHNSON DODGE

WHY CHEESECAKES CRACK

This Grand Canyon crack, which formed after refrigeration, indicates that the cheesecake spent too much time in the oven.

One of the most frequent and annoying problems with cheesecakes is that they can crack as they cool. It's difficult for cooks to believe the reason for that: It's overcooked. While the center may have still jiggled a bit while the cake was hot, after chilling you can usually see that the filling is firm and dry right around the crack. Overcooking causes proteins to shrink and the cake to dry out, leading to cracks.

The simplest way to avoid cracks is to shorten the cooking time, but you also can play with other variables. Sugar slows cooking by blocking the coagulation of proteins, so adding more provides an extra barrier against overcooking. Another option is to cut an egg out of the recipe. Fewer eggs mean fewer proteins, a slower rate of coagulation, and slower cooking.

If the unmentionable does occur and you end up with minor fissures in the cake, do what any resourceful cook would do: ice the cake with whipped cream and no one will ever know the difference.

Spiced Pumpkin Cheesecake with a
GINGERSNAP CRUST

This cheesecake is a luxurious twist on the traditional Thanksgiving pumpkin pie. Because a cheesecake needs at least a day to cool and set up, you can feel good about doing it a day or two ahead.

FOR THE CRUST:

About 40 gingersnap wafers (to yield 2 cups crumbs)

¼ cup packed light brown sugar

5 tablespoons unsalted butter, melted and cooled

FOR THE FILLING:

Four 8-ounce packages cream cheese, softened

1⅓ cups packed light brown sugar

1 teaspoon ground cinnamon

½ teaspoon ground ginger

¼ teaspoon ground allspice

¼ teaspoon freshly grated nutmeg

¼ teaspoon table salt

4 large eggs

2 large egg yolks

1 tablespoon pure vanilla extract

One 15-ounce can pure solid-pack pumpkin (not pumpkin pie filling)

Position a rack in the middle of the oven and heat the oven to 350°F.

MAKE THE CRUST: Pulse the cookies and brown sugar in a food processor until well combined and the crumbs are uniform. Transfer to a medium bowl; add the melted butter. Combine thoroughly, first with a spoon, then with your fingers, until the mixture is evenly moist, crumbly, and holds together when you squeeze a handful. Press the mixture evenly over the bottom and partway up the sides of a 9-inch springform pan. Chill for 5 minutes and then bake for 10 minutes. Let cool on a wire rack.

MAKE THE FILLING: Heat a kettle of water. In a stand mixer fitted with the paddle attachment (or in a large bowl with a hand mixer), beat the cream cheese until smooth. In a separate bowl, whisk the brown sugar, spices, and salt. Add this mixture to the cream cheese; beat until well blended, scraping down the sides of the bowl as needed. Add the whole eggs and yolks, one at a time, making sure each is thoroughly incorporated before adding the next and scraping the bowl after each. Blend in the vanilla and pumpkin.

Scrape the batter into the cooled crust. The batter will come up past the crust and fill the pan to the rim. Tap the pan gently once or twice on the counter to release any air bubbles. Set the pan in a larger baking dish (a roasting pan is good) and add enough hot water from the kettle to come about halfway up the sides of the springform pan. Bake until the top of the

(continued)

cake looks deep golden and burnished and the center is set (the cake may just barely begin to crack), 1 hour and 35 minutes to 1 hour and 45 minutes. The cake will still jiggle a little bit when tapped. The top may rise a bit but will settle as it cools.

Remove the cheesecake from the oven and carefully run a thin-bladed knife between the crust and the pan sides (this will prevent the cake from breaking as it cools). Let the cheesecake cool to room temperature in the pan on a wire rack. Cover and chill overnight.

—REGAN DALEY

HOW TO UNMOLD A CHEESECAKE
WITHOUT WRECKING IT

If you've used a springform pan, unmolding can be as easy as removing the ring. To remove the ring cleanly, follow the photos below.

If you want to remove the bottom of the pan as well, you can carefully transfer the cheesecake to a cake plate using two large spatulas or, for a very firm cheesecake, you can invert it twice (if you've used a cake pan instead of a springform, you'll have no choice but to do this). If you're planning to invert the cheesecake, it's a good idea to line the bottom of the greased pan with a round of greased parchment before baking.

Before unmolding the sides and bottom, be sure the cheesecake is thoroughly chilled (at least six hours in the refrigerator). Have ready a serving plate and another flat plate that's at least as wide as the springform and covered with plastic wrap. Remove the ring following the photos below. Set the plate with plastic wrap on top of the cheesecake and carefully invert the pan. Heat the base of the springform with a hot, damp cloth or a hair dryer, and lift it off. Peel away the parchment, if used. Set the serving plate lightly on the bottom of the cheesecake (which is now facing up) and reinvert the cake. Lift off the plastic-wrapped plate. If the cheesecake was baked without a crust, you may need to smooth the sides with a metal spatula.

To cut neat slices, use a sharp, thin-bladed knife dipped in hot water (shake off excess drops) between each slice. For a cheesecake without a crust, a piece of dental floss, held taut, also works (you'll need to cut across the diameter of the cake). —REGAN DALEY

Wipe a hot, damp cloth around the outside of the ring (or use a hair dryer).

Run a metal spatula or a thin knife inside the ring.

Release and gently loosen the ring, then lift it off.

ESPRESSO
Gingerbread Cake

YIELDS 1 LARGE BUNDT CAKE
OR 4 MINIATURE LOAVES

This cake has the homey appeal of classic gingerbread, but with a sophisticated kick from espresso and an espresso glaze. You can bake the cake, wrap it well (without glazing), and hold it for up to a week, glazing the day you plan to serve it.

½ cup dark molasses (not blackstrap)

½ cup very strong brewed coffee or espresso, cooled to just warm

11¼ ounces (2½ cups) all-purpose flour; more for the pan

2 teaspoons baking powder

½ teaspoon table salt

¼ teaspoon baking soda

1 tablespoon instant espresso powder

2 teaspoons ground ginger

½ teaspoon ground cinnamon

⅛ teaspoon ground nutmeg

⅛ teaspoon ground cloves

1¼ cups (2½ sticks) unsalted butter, softened; more for the pan

1¼ cups packed light brown sugar

3 large eggs, at room temperature

2 large egg yolks, at room temperature

Espresso Glaze (optional; page 185)

Position a rack in the middle of the oven and heat the oven to 350°F. Butter and flour a 10- or 12-cup Bundt® pan (or four 2-cup mini loaf pans). Tap out any excess flour.

In a liquid measuring cup, whisk together the molasses and coffee. In a medium bowl, sift together the flour, baking powder, salt, baking soda, espresso powder, and spices.

In a stand mixer fitted with the paddle attachment (or in a large bowl with a hand mixer), cream the butter on medium speed until smooth, about 1 minute. Add the brown sugar and beat until light and fluffy, about 2 minutes. Beat in the whole eggs and yolks one at a time, stopping to scrape the bowl after each addition. With the mixer on low speed, alternate adding the flour and coffee mixtures, beginning and ending with the flour. Stop the mixer at least one last time to scrape the bowl, then beat at medium speed until the batter is smooth, about 20 seconds.

Spoon the batter into the prepared pan, spreading it evenly with a rubber spatula. Run a knife through the batter to eliminate any air pockets or tap the pan lightly against the counter. Bake until a wooden skewer inserted in the center comes out clean, about 40 minutes (about 30 minutes for mini loaves). Set the pan on a wire rack to cool for 15 minutes. Invert the cake onto the rack, remove the pan, and let cool until just barely warm. Drizzle

with the glaze (if using) as directed below, then let cool to room temperature before serving. If you're making the cake ahead, wrap it while still barely warm without the glaze. If you plan to freeze the cake, don't glaze it until you're ready to serve it. —NICOLE REES

ESPRESSO GLAZE

1 cup confectioners' sugar

1 teaspoon dark rum (optional)

1½ tablespoons brewed espresso (or 1½ teaspoons instant espresso powder dissolved in 1½ tablespoons hot water)

YIELDS 1¼ CUPS

Combine the confectioners' sugar and rum (if using) in a bowl and, adding the espresso gradually, whisk until smooth. If necessary, add more espresso or water to thin the glaze to a drizzling consistency. When the cake is still barely warm, use a fork or spoon to drizzle the glaze over the top

PUMPKIN & GINGER
Pound Cake

SERVES 8, WITH AMPLE LEFTOVERS

This delicious twist on pumpkin pie will keep for two days at room temperature if wrapped tightly. You can also make it up to three weeks ahead. Wrap it first in plastic, then in foil, and freeze it; pull it out of the freezer four hours before serving.

1 cup (2 sticks) unsalted butter, completely softened; more for the pan

9½ ounces (2½ cups) cake flour; more for the pan

1½ teaspoons baking powder

½ teaspoon table salt

1½ teaspoons ground cinnamon

½ teaspoon ground ginger

¼ teaspoon freshly grated nutmeg

¼ teaspoon ground cloves

4 large eggs, at room temperature

2 teaspoons pure vanilla extract

2 cups packed light brown sugar

1 cup canned pure solid-pack pumpkin (not pumpkin pie filling)

¼ cup vegetable oil

2 teaspoons peeled and minced fresh ginger

1 to 2 tablespoons confectioners' sugar for dusting

1 quart vanilla ice cream (optional)

Position a rack in the lower third of the oven and heat the oven to 350°F. Butter and flour a 12-cup Bundt pan, preferably nonstick. Tap out any excess flour.

In a medium bowl, sift together the flour, baking powder, salt, and spices; set aside. Separate the eggs, putting the yolks in a small bowl and the whites in a large bowl.

In a stand mixer fitted with the whisk attachment (or in a large bowl with a hand mixer), cream the butter on medium speed until smooth, about 1 minute. On low speed, gradually add the vanilla and brown sugar, about ½ cup at a time. When all the brown sugar has been added, stop the mixer, scrape the bowl, and cream the mixture on medium speed until light and fluffy, 3 to 4 minutes.

Use a fork to lightly beat the egg yolks; then, with the mixer on low speed, add them slowly to the butter-sugar mixture. Scrape the bowl, increase the speed to medium, and beat for 1 minute. On low speed, add the pumpkin, oil, and fresh ginger. Beat until smooth. Using a rubber spatula, stir in one-third of the flour mixture and continue stirring just until the flour disappears (don't beat or overmix). Repeat, adding the remaining flour mixture in two more batches. Scrape the bowl and set it aside.

Add a pinch of salt to the egg whites and beat with a hand mixer with clean, dry beaters just until they hold soft peaks. Using a rubber spatula, gently but thoroughly fold them into the batter. Spoon the batter into the prepared pan, spreading it evenly with the rubber spatula. Run a knife through the batter to eliminate any air pockets or tap the pan lightly against the counter. Bake until the cake springs back when touched with a fingertip and a wooden skewer inserted into the center of the cake comes out mostly clean with a few moist crumbs clinging to it, 45 to 50 minutes. Set the pan on a wire rack to cool for 10 minutes and then carefully run a paring knife around the inside edge of the pan. Invert the cake onto the rack and gently remove the pan. Let cool completely. (If you're making ahead, wrap it now).

Just before serving, use a fine sieve to sift the confectioners' sugar over the cake. Cut into ¾-inch-thick slices and serve with a scoop of ice cream, if you like. —DIANE MORGAN

WHEN YOU DON'T HAVE THE RIGHT SIZE CAKE PAN

Sometimes you don't have the exact size and shape pan that's called for in a recipe, or perhaps you just want to try something different. If you follow these four tips, you can use whatever pan you want.

- Never fill the pan more than two-thirds of the way with batter. For full-size loaf or Bundt pans, leave over an inch of space at the top. For more than one pan, divide the batter evenly so the cakes bake at the same time.

- Keep the oven temperature the same for any size pan.

- Adjust your timing to fit the pan. Full-size Bundts take 40 to 50 minutes. Standard loaves take 45 to 50 minutes. Mini Bundts and mini loaves take anywhere from 20 to 35 minutes.

- Follow the signs of doneness, which are noted in all our cake recipes.

ORANGE
Layer Cake

YIELDS ONE 9-INCH LAYER CAKE; SERVES 8 TO 10

This old-fashioned layer cake makes a pretty and impressive finale to Thanksgiving dinner. It isn't a dessert that you can shake out of your sleeve, however. To manage the production, follow this timeline: The day before, make the filling and chill it, then make the cake layers and wrap in plastic. Thanksgiving morning, make the frosting and assemble the cake, and slice the oranges for the garnish. Do the final garnishing right before serving.

FOR THE FILLING:

⅔ cup granulated sugar

3 tablespoons all-purpose flour

1 cup strained fresh orange juice (from 3 large or 4 medium oranges)

2 large egg yolks

2 tablespoons salted butter

FOR THE CAKE:

2¼ cups (10⅛ ounces) all-purpose flour

2½ teaspoons baking powder

1 teaspoon table salt

⅓ cup salted butter

⅓ cup vegetable shortening

2 teaspoons grated orange zest (from about 1 large orange)

1½ cups granulated sugar

3 large eggs

1 cup strained fresh orange juice (from 3 large or 4 medium oranges)

FOR THE FROSTING:

¾ cup (1½ sticks) salted butter, softened

4½ cups (about 18 ounces) confectioners' sugar

Dash table salt

1 teaspoon grated orange zest

5 tablespoons fresh orange juice (from 1 large orange)

FOR THE GARNISH:

1 or 2 small oranges, thinly sliced, slices cut halfway through on one side, laid on paper towels to drain

7 or 8 sprigs fresh mint (pick pairs of leaves)

MAKE THE FILLING: Combine the granulated sugar and the flour in a medium, heavy-based saucepan. Whisk just to mix. Add the orange juice and egg yolks and whisk vigorously again to combine. Place over medium-high heat and cook, whisking constantly, until the mixture boils, 3 to 4 minutes. Cook another 1 minute, stirring constantly (the mixture will thicken noticeably and become less cloudy). Be sure it boils for 1 minute so that the filling thickens enough to support the cake. Remove from the heat and stir in the butter. Transfer to a bowl, cover with plastic wrap (lay the wrap directly on the filling's surface to keep a skin from forming) and refrigerate. Chill thoroughly before using.   *(continued)*

MAKE THE CAKE: Heat the oven to 350°F. Grease two 9x1½-inch cake pans and line the bottom of each with a round of parchment. Lightly flour the sides and bottom of each pan. In a medium bowl, sift together the flour, baking powder, and salt. In a stand mixer fitted with the paddle attachment (or in a large bowl with a hand mixer), cream the butter, shortening, and orange zest. Gradually add the granulated sugar, creaming until the mixture is light and fluffy. Scrape the sides of the bowl. Add the eggs, one at a time, mixing well after each addition and scraping the bowl. Add the dry ingredients alternately with the orange juice, beating well on low speed after each addition. Pour equal amounts of the batter into the two prepared cake pans. Run a knife through the batter to eliminate any air pockets or tap the pans lightly on the counter. Bake until a wooden skewer inserted in the center comes out clean, about 28 minutes. Let cool in the pans on a wire rack for 10 minutes and then loosen the layers by running a knife between the cake and the edge of the pan. Remove the layers from the pans and put them on the rack to continue cooling.

MAKE THE FROSTING: Cream the butter in a stand mixer (or in a large bowl with a hand mixer). Add the confectioners' sugar and salt and combine thoroughly. Add the orange zest and mix to combine. Add the orange juice and mix on high speed until well blended, scraping the bowl. The frosting will be light and creamy. Refrigerate if not using right away.

ASSEMBLE THE CAKE: When all the components are cool, put one cake layer on a cake stand or a cardboard cake round. Spread the orange filling over the cake to make a ¼-inch-thick layer; see the photo at right. You'll have about ⅓ cup extra filling; serve it alongside the cake, if you like. Put the second layer on top of the first and refrigerate the cake until the filling has chilled again and firmed up, about 45 minutes. Loosen the frosting by beating it with a rubber spatula (if it's very stiff, beat it with a hand mixer). Using an icing spatula, spread just a very thin layer of frosting over the whole cake (this is called a "crumb coat" because it secures any loose crumbs) and refrigerate the cake to let the frosting firm up, about 10 minutes. Put on the final coat of frosting, taking care to work gently, as the top layer of the cake tends to slide around ever so slightly because of the filling. If it slides, just push it back. Create a pattern on the frosting using the icing spatula (heat it up under warm water and dry it). Transfer the cake (on its cardboard or by lifting it with spatulas) to a cake plate or pedestal.

GARNISH THE CAKE: Twist the orange slices into S shapes and put seven or eight around the top of the cake. Tuck a pair of mint leaves into each orange twist. —RIS LACOSTE

FILLING AND FROSTING
AN OLD-FASHIONED LAYER CAKE

Paying attention to the details yields lovely results

Start in the center and spread gently until the filling is ¼ inch thick and a bit shy of the edge. Chill before frosting.

Try this pro's trick: Spread a very thin layer of frosting to pick up any stray crumbs. Chill to firm up and then finish with a second, thicker layer of frosting.

A sweeping motion with an offset spatula makes a pretty pattern. This decoration is easy even for cake novices.

Tiramisu

SERVES 10 TO 12

This traditional Italian coffee-and-cocoa dessert is both special-occasion and comfort food at the same time, perfect for Thanksgiving. Texture is key to tiramisù; the ladyfingers must be just barely soaked through with coffee, so use the crisp, cookie-style ladyfingers, rather than the sponge-cake style. This recipe calls for uncooked eggs, so keep the tiramisù refrigerated and serve it within 48 hours. If the uncooked eggs in this dish are a concern, use pasteurized eggs.

5 cups hot brewed espresso (or double-strength drip coffee made with espresso roast)

1 cup plus 2 tablespoons granulated sugar

2 tablespoons rum, or more to taste (optional)

4 large eggs, separated

16 ounces (2 cups) mascarpone cheese

About 46 ladyfingers or savoiardi cookies, preferably Balocco, Bonomi, or Elledi brand

2 tablespoons unsweetened cocoa powder or 1 to 2 ounces bittersweet chocolate, finely chopped (see How to Chop Chocolate, page 194)

Pour the coffee in a large bowl and add 2 tablespoons of the sugar while it's still hot. Stir well and let cool to room temperature. Add the rum, if using.

Combine the egg yolks and the remaining 1 cup sugar in a stand mixer fitted with the whisk attachment (or in a large bowl if using a hand mixer). Beat on medium-high speed until the yolks are pale yellow and fluffy, about 5 minutes. (The mixture will be fairly thick at first.) Add the mascarpone and beat until it's fully incorporated into a smooth cream, 2 to 3 minutes more. If using a stand mixer, transfer the mixture to a large bowl.

Thoroughly wash and dry the beaters and the stand mixer bowl, if using. Put the egg whites in a medium bowl or the stand mixer bowl and whip on medium-high speed until they form medium-stiff peaks when you lift the beaters (the tips should curl over onto themselves just a little). With a large rubber spatula, fold about one-quarter of the beaten whites into the mascarpone cream to lighten it. Then gently fold in the remaining whites, taking care not to deflate them. Cover with plastic wrap and refrigerate.

Submerge one ladyfinger in the cooled coffee until the coffee penetrates about halfway through, leaving the core dry (break it to check, see photo, page 195). This can take from 1 to 12 seconds, depending on the type of ladyfinger. You don't want the ladyfinger to get completely soaked or it will become soggy and fall apart. You should be able to feel that the outside is soft, but the inside is still firm.

Once you've determined the correct soaking time, submerge each ladyfinger individually, gently shake off excess coffee, and immediately set it in a 9x13-inch baking dish; continue until you have one tight layer that covers the bottom of the dish. (You

(continued)

may need to break a few ladyfingers to fit in snugly.) Spread one-half of the mascarpone cream evenly on top of the ladyfingers. Repeat the soaking procedure with the remaining ladyfingers to create a second snug layer, arranging them on top of the mascarpone cream as you did for the first layer. Spread the rest of the mascarpone cream evenly on top. Cover the dish with plastic wrap and refrigerate for at least 2 hours.

Before serving, sift the cocoa powder or grated chocolate over the top to evenly cover.

— LAURA GIANNATEMPO

HOW TO CHOP CHOCOLATE

If you plan to melt chocolate, you'll have less chance of scorching it if you first chop it as evenly as possible. When chopping chocolate, the tiny shards inevitably get everywhere. For easy cleanup, line a rimmed baking sheet with parchment and put your cutting board on top of that. Use the paper to gather the shards.

To chop a thick slab of chocolate, set the blade of your biggest knife (preferably a chef's knife) on a corner of the slab and bear down with both hands to break off a small bit; repeat. As that corner becomes a flat edge, turn the slab and begin cutting at another point.

For chopping large amounts of chocolate, a food processor can work. Break thin bars into pieces and pulse in the processor with the steel blade until it's evenly chopped. Sometimes a few pieces resist chopping; break these into smaller pieces and keep pulsing. For block chocolate, cut the block into chunks that will fit in the feed tube and use the coarse grating disk (heavy block chocolate might damage the machine if you use the steel blade).

— ABIGAIL JOHNSON DODGE

A LUSCIOUS ITALIAN CLASSIC
THAT'S EASY TO ASSEMBLE

Break one ladyfinger after you've dipped it in the cooled coffee to check that the coffee has penetrated only halfway through, leaving the core dry. The outside will be quite soft, but the inside should be firm.

Evenly spread half the mascarpone cream with a spatula over a tight layer of ladyfingers arranged in a 9x13-inch baking dish.

Use a fine sieve to finish off the tiramisù with a generous dusting of cocoa powder just before serving.

PUMPKIN
Bread Pudding | YIELDS 6 TO 8

This rich, satisfying pudding is lovely by itself, but the crème fraîche garnish adds a tangy-smooth complement. Because this cooks in a water bath, it requires a bit of oven space, so you could bake it in the morning and gently reheat it before serving; it should be served just barely warm.

1 tablespoon unsalted butter, softened

¼ cup granulated sugar

1 large loaf (1 to 1½ pounds) day-old challah or other soft, eggy bread

½ cup dried cranberries or golden raisins

1½ cups whole milk

1½ cups heavy cream

⅔ cup packed light brown sugar

1 teaspoon ground cinnamon

½ teaspoon freshly grated nutmeg

½ teaspoon table salt

3 large eggs

3 large egg yolks

1 cup canned pure solid-pack pumpkin (not pumpkin pie filling)

1 teaspoon pure vanilla extract

8 ounces (1 cup) crème fraîche, for garnish (optional)

Heat a kettle of water. Position a rack in the middle of the oven and heat the oven to 350°F. With the softened butter, grease a 2½-quart ceramic baking dish or casserole that's 3 inches deep. Dust the inside with 2 tablespoons of the granulated sugar. Tap out and discard the excess.

Trim the ends off the bread and cut the rest into ½- to ⅔-inch-thick slices. Cut the slices in half from top to bottom and arrange them in the prepared dish in overlapping rows or circles, stopping when the dish is full. Scatter the cranberries over the bread.

Combine the milk and cream in a 2-quart, heavy-based saucepan over medium-high heat. Bring just to a boil and then remove from the heat. In a large bowl, whisk the brown sugar, cinnamon, nutmeg, and salt. Whisk in the whole eggs and yolks. Blend in the pumpkin and vanilla. Wrap a damp kitchen towel around the base of the bowl to hold it steady. Whisking constantly, gradually pour in the hot milk-cream mixture. Pour the warm custard over the bread in the baking dish, making sure to soak each piece of bread completely. Gently press down on the bread to even the top of the pudding and to ensure that each slice is saturated. Sprinkle the pudding with the remaining 2 tablespoons granulated sugar.

Set the baking dish into a larger pan (a roasting pan is good). Set the pan on the oven rack and add enough hot water from the kettle to come halfway up the sides of the baking dish. Bake until the top is light golden and crusty and the pudding feels firm, 45 to 60 minutes. Let the pudding cool in its water bath on a wire rack. Serve warm or at room temperature in shallow bowls with generous dollops of crème fraîche, if using. Leftovers can be covered and refrigerated for up to three days; warm in a 325°F oven before serving, if you like. —REGAN DALEY

CRISP
Pear Strudel

SERVES 6 TO 8

Despite this strudel's delicate appearance, it holds and reheats very nicely, so you can assemble and bake it the morning of Thanksgiving and then reheat it right before serving. Phyllo is available in the freezer section of most supermarkets. Put the package in the refrigerator the day before you plan to use it; it must thaw slowly. As you work, cover the phyllo sheets with a damp dishtowel, which will keep them pliable.

2 cups water

2 cups granulated sugar

½ vanilla bean, halved lengthwise and seeded (with a paring knife); reserve the seeds for another use (or 1 teaspoon pure vanilla extract)

2 strips lemon zest

4 slices fresh ginger, each ⅛ inch thick

Juice of 1 lemon (about 2 tablespoons)

4 ripe Bartlett pears, peeled, cored, and sliced lengthwise into 8 pieces each

⅓ cup golden raisins

2 tablespoons Cognac

⅓ cup whole, skin-on almonds

4 sheets frozen phyllo dough, thawed

½ cup (1 stick) unsalted butter, melted

½ cup coarsely crushed amaretti cookies, or stale breadcrumbs

Confectioners' sugar for sprinkling

In a medium saucepan over high heat, combine the water and granulated sugar and bring to a boil, stirring to dissolve the sugar. Add the vanilla bean, lemon zest, and ginger. Reduce the heat to low and simmer for 10 minutes. Add the lemon juice and pears (and vanilla extract, if using). Cover and poach gently until the pears are soft, about 15 minutes.

Refrigerate the pears in the liquid for at least 2 and up to 24 hours. Put the raisins in a small bowl, cover with the Cognac, and also let soak in the refrigerator for the same amount of time.

Heat the oven to 325°F. Position a rack in the middle of the oven. On a small baking sheet, toast the almonds until golden brown in the center, about 12 minutes. Let cool, then chop coarsely and set aside.

Increase the oven temperature to 400°F. Set the pears in a colander to drain (it's fine to discard the syrup).

Put a clean, damp (but not wet) dishtowel on the counter and gently lay the phyllo sheets on top. Cover with a second damp towel (this will keep the pastry from drying out). Cover your workspace with a piece of parchment slightly larger than the phyllo sheets. Remove two phyllo sheets and lay them on top of the parchment with one of the longest side facing you. Brush generously with melted butter, then sprinkle with half of the toasted almonds. Lay the other two phyllo sheets on top and repeat. Sprinkle the amaretti crumbs or breadcrumbs in a band about 2 inches wide along the edge closest to you. Arrange the pears on top of the crumbs and sprinkle with the raisins.

Starting at the edge closest to you and using the parchment as an aid, gently roll up the strudel and set it on a parchment-lined baking sheet. With a serrated knife, score the top at about 2-inch intervals. Bake for 20 minutes, then lower the oven temperature to 350°F, and continue to bake until the pastry is a deep golden brown, 10 to 15 minutes. Let cool and store at room temperature until ready to serve. To serve, reheat in a 350°F oven until warm and then sprinkle with the confectioners' sugar. —ARLENE JACOBS

THE SECRET TO PHYLLO: KEEP IT MOIST

Phyllo pastry undeservedly strikes fear in the hearts of many cooks. It shouldn't: It's forgiving if you work with it properly. You can usually find it in your market's frozen food aisle. Since phyllo dries out quickly, try to buy it fairly fresh. Check the expiration date or buy from a store with quick turnover. Put the package in the fridge the day before you plan to use it to be sure it thaws. And—most important—as you work, keep the phyllo covered with a damp dishtowel, which will keep it pliable.

APPLE-CRANBERRY *Crisp*

SERVES 6 TO 8

You can bake this buttery, crunchy crisp in individual baking dishes if you'd like a more formal presentation. The pecan topping can be made up to three days ahead and kept in an airtight container in the fridge. You can even prepare the apple filling, put it in the baking dish, and refrigerate it up to 6 hours ahead, adding the pecan topping just before baking. If the filling is cold, allow a few more minutes cooking time.

3 pounds apples (4 to 5 medium-large), such as Braeburn, Gala, Rome, or Honeycrisp

½ teaspoon ground cinnamon

½ pound (2¼ cups) fresh cranberries, picked over and rinsed

1 teaspoon finely grated orange zest

1 tablespoon unsalted butter

3 tablespoons fresh orange juice

Pinch table salt

1 cup granulated sugar

Pecan Topping (page 201)

Heat the oven to 375°F. Butter the sides only of a 9-inch-square baking pan.

Peel, quarter, and core the apples. Cut each apple quarter crosswise into ¾-inch-thick slices. Put them in a large bowl, sprinkle on the cinnamon, and toss until evenly coated. Combine the cranberries and orange zest in a food processor and pulse until the cranberries are finely chopped, scraping the sides with a rubber spatula as needed. Add the cranberries to the apples and toss to combine.

Put the butter, orange juice, and salt in a small microwaveable dish or a small pan. Heat in the microwave or over medium-low heat until the butter melts, about 1 minute. Swirl to blend, then pour over the apples, and toss to coat. Add the sugar and toss to coat again. Pour the apple mixture into the prepared pan and spread it evenly. Sprinkle the topping evenly on top of the apples.

Line a heavy-duty rimmed baking sheet with foil. Set the pan on the sheet and bake until the juices are bubbling on the sides, the top is golden brown, crisp, and hard, and the apples are tender when pierced with a fork, 60 to 70 minutes (rotate the pan for even browning, if necessary). If the top starts to get too brown after 45 minutes, cover it loosely with foil. Let cool on a wire rack for at least 30 minutes so the juices thicken. Serve warm. —WENDY KALEN

PECAN TOPPING

5¾ ounces (1¼ cups) all-purpose flour

½ cup firmly packed light brown sugar

2 tablespoons granulated sugar

½ teaspoon ground cinnamon

¼ teaspoon table salt

½ cup (1 stick) cold unsalted butter, cut into ½-inch pieces

3 ounces (¾ cup) pecans, coarsely chopped

In a medium bowl, combine the flour, both sugars, cinnamon, and salt. Rub in the butter with your fingertips until it's well blended and the mixture is clumpy but still a bit crumbly (it should hold together if you pinch it). Mix in the pecans. Refrigerate until ready to use.

BLACK FOREST
Trifle
SERVES 16

A trifle is one of those dishes that's so old-fashioned, it feels brand-new again. Not that many people make them anymore, but they should, because they're easy to do ahead and yet they're real show-stoppers, especially if you have a footed glass trifle bowl. Any attractive clear bowl will work, however. You'll need one that can accommodate 2½ to 3 quarts. A trifle actually benefits from being prepared in advance, which allows the flavors to meld. Make it a few hours ahead and leave in the fridge, or make the cake and syrup up to a day ahead. Wrap the cake and keep it at room temperature, and cover and refrigerate the syrup.

FOR THE CAKE:

2 ounces semisweet chocolate, chopped (see How to Chop Chocolate, page 194)

1 ounce unsweetened chocolate, chopped

5 ounces (1 cup plus 2 tablespoons) all-purpose flour

2 tablespoons unsweetened Dutch-processed cocoa powder

½ teaspoon baking powder

½ teaspoon baking soda

¼ teaspoon table salt

6 tablespoons (¾ stick) unsalted butter, softened

1 cup granulated sugar

2 large eggs

1 teaspoon pure vanilla extract

½ cup sour cream

⅓ cup strong brewed coffee

FOR THE CHERRIES AND KIRSCH SYRUP:

One 15- or 16-ounce can pitted sweet cherries in heavy or extra-heavy syrup

¼ cup kirsch (cherry brandy)

Granulated sugar to taste

FOR THE WHIPPED CREAM:

3 cups cold heavy cream

½ cup granulated sugar

1 tablespoon kirsch

FOR ASSEMBLING THE TRIFLE:

1 cup semisweet chocolate shavings (from a 3- to 4-ounce block of chocolate; use a vegetable peeler to do this)

TO MAKE THE CAKE: Position a rack in the middle of the oven and heat the oven to 350°F. Butter the bottom and sides of a 9x2-inch round cake pan. Line the bottom of the pan with a round of parchment and butter the parchment.

Fill a medium skillet with about ½ inch water and heat until just below a simmer. Put both the semisweet and unsweetened chocolates in a medium heatproof bowl and set the bowl in the barely simmering water. Stir until the chocolate is melted and smooth. Remove from the water bath and let cool slightly.

(continued)

In a small bowl, sift together the flour, cocoa, baking powder, baking soda, and salt. In a stand mixer fitted with the paddle attachment (or in a large bowl with a hand mixer), beat the butter and sugar on medium speed until light and fluffy, 2 to 4 minutes. Mix in the slightly cooled melted chocolate on low speed just until incorporated. Increase the speed to medium and add the eggs one at a time, beating well after each addition. Scrape the sides of the bowl, add the vanilla, and beat on medium speed for another minute. On low speed, mix in the sour cream just until it's incorporated. Add the flour mixture (in three additions), alternating with the coffee (in two additions); scrape the bowl as needed. The batter will be very thick, like chocolate mousse or frosting.

Scrape the batter into the prepared pan and smooth the top. Bake until the top feels firm and a wooden skewer inserted in the center comes out clean, about 35 minutes. The cake may sink a bit in the center, but that's fine. Let the cake cool for 20 minutes in the baking pan on a wire rack. Using a small, sharp knife, loosen the sides of the cake from the pan, invert the cake onto the rack, and discard the paper liner. Let cool completely.

TO PREPARE THE CHERRIES: Drain the cherries in a colander set over a large bowl (to catch the syrup) for 30 minutes. Reserve ½ cup of the syrup. Transfer the cherries to a small bowl, drizzle with 1 tablespoon of the kirsch, and set aside. Taste the syrup; it should be slightly tart and not too sweet. If necessary, stir in 1 to 2 teaspoons sugar. Put the syrup in a small saucepan and simmer over medium heat until reduced by about half, about 3 minutes. Remove the pan from the heat and stir in the remaining 3 tablespoons kirsch. Set aside to cool.

Put the cream, sugar, and kirsch in a large bowl and, with an electric mixer, whip on high speed until it holds firm peaks.

TO ASSEMBLE THE TRIFLE: When you're ready to assemble the trifle, pick out the ten best-looking cherries and blot them dry with paper towels. With a long, serrated knife, cut the cooled cake vertically (all the way across the cake) into ½-inch-thick slices. Line the bottom of a 2½- to 3-quart glass bowl or trifle bowl with about a third of the cake slices to create an even layer. Don't worry if the pieces break, as long as they fill in the spaces. Brush this layer of cake lightly with some of the kirsch syrup, top with a third of the whipped cream, and randomly nestle half of the remaining cherries into the cream. Sprinkle with a third of the chocolate shavings. Repeat with two more layers. On the top layer of cream, arrange the best-looking cherries in a ring near the rim of the bowl and scatter the chocolate shavings inside the cherry ring. Refrigerate for at least 30 minutes and up to 6 hours. Serve chilled. —ELINOR KLIVANS

INDIVIDUAL
Mocha Soufflés | SERVES 6

The great thing about these soufflés is that you must *prepare them ahead so that they're chilled before they go in the oven. You can make and keep them in the refrigerator for up to 24 hours or the freezer up to two weeks. If you plan to bake them the same day you make them, don't use the full 3 tablespoons of rum or brandy; use only 1½ tablespoons plus 1½ tablespoons of water. Otherwise the alcohol flavor (which dissipates over time) will be too strong.*

6 tablespoons (¾ stick) unsalted butter, cut into pieces; more for the ramekins

Granulated sugar for dusting

3 tablespoons dark rum, brandy, Grand Marnier, or water

1½ teaspoons instant coffee granules

6 ounces bittersweet chocolate, finely chopped (see How to Chop Chocolate, page 194)

¼ teaspoon table salt

3 large eggs, separated and at room temperature

¾ cup confectioners' sugar

Lightly butter six 6-ounce ramekins and dust with granulated sugar, tapping out the excess. Set the ramekins on a small baking sheet.

Stir together the liquor or water and the coffee. Set aside and stir occasionally until the coffee is dissolved.

Melt the chocolate and 6 tablespoons butter together in a microwave or in a large metal bowl set over a pan of simmering water. Remove from the heat and whisk until glossy and smooth. Stir in the coffee mixture and the salt. Whisk in the egg yolks, one at a time. Add about one-third of the confectioners' sugar and whisk until well blended and smooth. Set aside.

In a medium bowl, beat the egg whites with a hand mixer on medium-high speed until they're very foamy and just beginning to hold soft peaks. Increase the speed to high and gradually sprinkle in the remaining confectioners' sugar. Continue beating until the peaks are firm and *(continued)*

glossy. Spoon about one-quarter of the beaten whites into the chocolate mixture and whisk until blended. Add the remaining whites and gently fold them in with a large rubber spatula until just blended. Pour evenly into the prepared ramekins (the mixture will almost completely fill the ramekins). If you want to bake the soufflés within 24 hours, refrigerate them. (To refrigerate, chill for about 30 minutes, then cover with plastic and return to the refrigerator for up to 24 hours.) If you want to hold them for longer, freeze them. (To freeze, put the filled ramekins in the freezer, uncovered, for 20 minutes. Then wrap each ramekin well in plastic and freeze for up to two weeks.)

TO BAKE STRAIGHT FROM THE REFRIGERATOR: Heat the oven to 400°F. Unwrap the ramekins, set them on a baking sheet, and bake until they've puffed and risen about 1 inch above the ramekin, about 15 minutes. The top will still be slightly sunken in the center; consider it a place to pop in a few berries or a dollop of whipped cream. Remove the soufflés from the oven and serve immediately.

TO BAKE STRAIGHT FROM THE FREEZER: Unwrap the ramekins and set them on a baking sheet. Let them sit for 20 minutes while heating the oven to 400°F. Bake on the baking sheet until they've puffed and risen about 1 inch above the ramekin, about 18 minutes. Remove from the oven and serve immediately. —ABIGAIL JOHNSON DODGE

BAKING SOUFFLÉS FROM THE FREEZER

Depending on how cold your freezer is, the soufflés may be slightly more or less done in 18 minutes. They'll be delicious either way. If they're a little underdone, they'll be a bit runny in the center; if a little overdone, they'll be a bit cakey in the center. It's best to stick to 18 minutes, as you don't want to use a method to test doneness that might deflate the soufflés. After you've made this recipe once in your own kitchen, you can adjust the timing as you like.

White Chocolate Soufflé Cakes
WITH RASPBERRY-
CHOCOLATE SAUCE | SERVES 6

Could there be a more ingenious dessert recipe? A moist and melt-in-your mouth cake, with all the airy mystique of a soufflé, that makes its own luxurious chocolate sauce...and you can make it two days ahead.

Softened unsalted butter and granulated sugar for the ramekins

FOR THE RASPBERRY-CHOCOLATE SAUCE:

½ cup fresh raspberries, rinsed, or ¾ cup thawed frozen raspberries

3 ounces bittersweet or semisweet chocolate, chopped (see How to Chop Chocolate, page 194)

2 tablespoons unsalted butter

1 tablespoon granulated sugar

FOR THE SOUFFLÉ CAKES:

3 large eggs, separated and at room temperature

3 tablespoons all-purpose flour

⅛ teaspoon table salt

¾ cup whole milk

6 ounces white chocolate (El Rey or Callebaut are good brands), finely chopped

¼ teaspoon pure vanilla extract

Scant ¼ teaspoon cream of tartar

2 tablespoons granulated sugar

Put a metal or Pyrex pie plate or cake pan in the freezer to chill. Lightly butter six 6-ounce ramekins or custard cups. Coat with sugar.

MAKE THE SAUCE: Purée the raspberries in a food processor, then transfer it to a fine sieve set over a small bowl. Strain the purée by pressing and scraping with a rubber spatula.

In a medium heatproof bowl set in or over a skillet of barely simmering water, combine the chocolate, butter, sugar, and 2 tablespoons of the raspberry purée (save any extra for another use). Stir frequently with a rubber spatula until melted and smooth. Scrape into a puddle on the chilled plate and return to the freezer until firm, 20 to 30 minutes. When the raspberry-chocolate mixture is firm, use a teaspoon to scrape it into six rough balls. Keep the balls on the plate and refrigerate until ready to use.

(continued)

MAKE THE SOUFFLÉ CAKES: Put the egg yolks in a medium bowl near the stove and have another large, clean bowl at hand. Combine the flour and salt in a small, heavy-based saucepan. Whisk in just enough of the milk to make a smooth paste. Whisk in the remaining milk. Set the pan over medium heat and cook, whisking constantly, until the mixture has the consistency of a thick cream sauce, 2 to 3 minutes. Whisk about 2 tablespoons of the hot sauce into the yolks to warm them up gently. Scrape the yolks back into the saucepan and cook for a minute or two, whisking constantly, until the mixture becomes a thick pastry cream; it should be about as thick as store-bought mayonnaise. Use a rubber spatula to scrape the pastry cream into the clean bowl. Add the white chocolate and whisk until it's fully melted and incorporated. Stir in the vanilla. Set aside for a few minutes until tepid.

In a stand mixer fitted with the whisk attachment (or in a large bowl with a hand mixer), beat the egg whites and cream of tartar on medium speed until the whites mound gently. Gradually beat in the sugar and beat until the whites form medium-stiff peaks when you lift the beaters; the tips should curl over but still look moist, glossy, and flexible (see the photo at right). With a large rubber spatula, fold about one-quarter of the whites into the white chocolate pastry cream to lighten it. Scrape the remaining whites into the bowl and gently fold in until blended, taking care not to deflate the whites.

Take the chocolate balls out of the refrigerator and put one in the center of each ramekin. Divide the batter evenly among the ramekins and level the tops gently with the back of a spoon. You can now heat the oven and bake right away or cover the ramekins with plastic and refrigerate for up to two days.

When you're ready to bake, position a rack in the lower third of the oven and heat the oven to 375°F. Remove the plastic and put the ramekins on a baking sheet. Bake until the cakes are puffed and golden brown on top—they'll quiver when tapped and seem soft in the center, 16 to 18 minutes. Let cool for a few minutes before serving. —ALICE MEDRICH

Tip

If you've beaten your egg whites properly, they should look like those in the photo (medium-stiff peaks whose tips curl when the beaters are lifted). But if you overbeat your egg whites—to the point that they clump instead of blend when you fold them—there is a fix: First, use a clean spatula to scoop a quarter of the whites into the batter. If the whites clump badly instead of blend as you fold, beat a fresh egg white into the remaining whites for a few seconds to remoisten them—they won't be perfect, but they should soften up. You can now fold the revived whites into your batter.

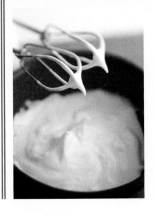

THE SECRET TO A HIDDEN SAUCE

*Putting a lump of chilled chocolate sauce in the ramekin before
baking the soufflé cakes solves the problem some molten cakes suffer from when
overbaked: the middle firms up rather than pools. You can also play with different
flavorings in the chocolate, for example orange liqueur, raspberry purée, or espresso.*

Start by pouring a mixture of melted chocolate and butter into a puddle on a pie plate. Freeze until firm, then use a teaspoon to scoop into six rough balls.

Put one chocolate ball in the center of each ramekin and spoon the batter on top. As the cakes bake, the chocolate melts into a warm, sumptuous sauce.

chapter

8

Continuing
the Feast

For some people, the day *after* Thanksgiving is when the fun really begins. From soothing soups to chile-spiked Mexican-inspired dishes to hearty pastas (and no turkey tetrazzini in sight), turkey's obligingly mild flavor adapts to all kinds of dishes. Plan to roast a little more bird than you need for the main meal so you'll have the chance to enjoy our second-day but first-rate recipes.

ROASTED
Turkey Stock

YIELDS ABOUT 9 CUPS

Simmering the turkey carcass after Thanksgiving is one of the rituals of the season—it's peaceful, it's practical, and it makes the house smell great. Stock from roasted bones will be more subtle than that made from raw bones and meat, but it lends good background flavor to lighter soups and braises. This stock freezes well (portion it into smaller containers for easy thawing), and turkey stock can, of course, always be used in place of chicken stock. If your turkey is larger than the bird listed below, just add more vegetables and other flavorings and use two stockpots.

2 tablespoons vegetable oil

Turkey carcass from a 12- to 16-pound bird
(plus bones and wings, if saved)

1 large onion (unpeeled), halved

2 ribs celery, coarsely chopped

1 large carrot, coarsely chopped

¼ cup brandy

One 1-inch chunk fresh ginger, peeled
and sliced

1 bay leaf

1 sprig fresh thyme

10 black peppercorns

About 12 cups cold water

Position a rack in the middle of the oven and heat to 425°F.

Pour the oil into a large flameproof roasting pan. Break or chop the turkey carcass into three or four pieces and put it in the pan, along with the onion, celery, and carrot. Roast for 30 minutes, stirring two or three times to ensure even browning. Transfer the turkey and vegetables to a large stockpot.

Pour off and discard any fat from the roasting pan, set the pan over medium heat, and add the brandy. Stir with a wooden spoon, scraping up all the browned bits from the bottom of the pan. When the mixture is bubbling, pour the drippings into the stockpot. Add the ginger, bay leaf, thyme, and peppercorns to the pot. Add the water (or enough to almost cover the turkey pieces). Bring to a simmer, skim any foam that rises to the top, and then reduce the heat to a very slow simmer. Simmer for 2 hours (if you used more than 12 cups water, you may need to boil it down a bit further for flavor).

Strain the stock into a large bowl, let cool, and refrigerate overnight. The next day, skim the fat from the surface and portion the stock for future use. —JENNIFER MCLAGAN

Turkey Soup with
GINGER, LEMON & MINT

SERVES 4 AS A FIRST COURSE; YIELDS 5 CUPS

The combination of ginger, lemon, and mint gives this soup a light, bright flavor. You could substitute cooked chicken for the turkey.

3 leeks (white part only), sliced ¼ inch thick (2 cups)

4½ cups Roasted Turkey Stock (page 212)

2 carrots, peeled and sliced ¼ inch thick

One 1-inch chunk fresh ginger, peeled and cut into matchsticks (about 2 tablespoons)

1 cup diced (½-inch) cooked turkey

2 tablespoons fresh lemon juice

½ teaspoon kosher salt

Freshly ground black pepper

¼ cup finely shredded fresh mint

Put the sliced leeks in a large bowl of cold water and let them soak for 10 minutes. Lift them out carefully, making sure to leave the grit at the bottom of the bowl behind, and set aside (there's no need to dry them).

Put the stock and carrots in a large saucepan. Bring to a boil, reduce the heat, and cover the pot. Simmer for 5 minutes and then add the leeks and ginger. Continue to cook, covered, until the vegetables are just tender, about another 5 minutes. Add the turkey, lemon juice, salt, and pepper. Simmer until the turkey is heated through, about 2 minutes. Adjust the seasonings if needed, add the mint, and serve immediately.

—JENNIFER MCLAGAN

TURKEY
Tortilla Soup

Soup isn't an unusual destination for leftover roast turkey, but this Mexican-style soup is anything but ordinary, bursting with all sorts of interesting flavors and textures. You can make it as light or as hearty as you want, just by varying the amount of added ingredients, such as beans and corn, and the garnishes.

FOR THE SOUP:

1 tablespoon vegetable oil; plus 1½ to 2 cups for frying the tortilla strips

½ cup finely diced yellow onion

1½ tablespoons chili powder

1 tablespoon tomato paste

4 cups Roasted Turkey Stock (page 212) or homemade or low-salt chicken broth

6 fresh cilantro sprigs

Kosher salt

Three 6-inch corn tortillas, cut into ¼-inch-wide strips

1 cup shredded or diced cooked turkey

¾ cup diced (½-inch) fresh tomato or quartered cherry tomatoes

½ cup cooked fresh or frozen corn kernels

½ cup canned black beans, rinsed and drained

FOR THE GARNISH:

½ to 1 ripe avocado, cut into ½-inch dice

¼ cup crumbled queso fresco or feta

3 tablespoons chopped fresh cilantro

2 tablespoons sour cream, or to taste (optional)

½ lime, cut into wedges

Heat the 1 tablespoon oil in a medium saucepan over medium heat. Add the onion and cook, stirring occasionally with a wooden spoon, until softened and just beginning to brown, 3 to 4 minutes. Add the chili powder and tomato paste and cook, stirring, for 15 to 30 seconds; don't let the chili powder scorch. Pour in the stock and scrape the bottom of the pan with the spoon to loosen any browned bits. Add the cilantro sprigs and bring to a boil over medium-high heat. Reduce the heat to medium low and simmer, uncovered, until the stock has reduced by about a third and is very flavorful, 20 to 30 minutes. Discard the cilantro sprigs and season to taste with salt.

While the stock reduces, fry the tortilla strips. Line a plate or tray with two layers of paper towels. Pour 1 inch of oil into a small, high-sided saucepan (a 6-inch-diameter pan needs about 1½ cups of oil). If you have a candy thermometer, attach it to the pot. Heat the oil over medium heat until it reaches 350°F, or until a tortilla strip sizzles immediately when dipped into the oil. Add 8 to 10 tortilla strips and scrunch them with tongs for a few seconds to give them a wavy shape. Fry until the bubbling subsides and the strips are crisp and very lightly browned, about 1 minute. Transfer to the paper towels to drain and sprinkle with a little salt while they're still hot. Repeat with the remaining strips.

Divide the turkey, tomato, corn, beans, and tortilla strips between two large soup bowls. If necessary, reheat the stock until it's piping hot. Pour the stock over the ingredients in the bowls. Garnish with the avocado, cheese, chopped cilantro, dollops of sour cream (if using), and big squeezes of lime juice. Serve immediately. — ADAPTED FROM MARTHA HOLMBERG

Turkey & Fall Vegetable in a
SAFFRON-SCENTED BROTH
WITH COUSCOUS

SERVES 4

Couscous is traditionally served with harissa, a chile sauce that isn't readily available. Instead, this recipe uses the Indonesian chile paste sambal oelek, which is an easier-to-find substitute and available in Asian markets, or you can substitute a few shakes of hot sauce. This recipe is easily doubled.

Generous pinch saffron threads

¼ teaspoon turmeric

One 3-inch-long cinnamon stick

1 fresh hot red chile (like a serrano), cored, seeded, and quartered

3 cups Roasted Turkey Stock (page 212)

1 medium red onion, root end left intact, cut into wedges about ¾ inch thick at the widest side

2 medium carrots, peeled and cut into 1½ x ¾-inch sticks

2 medium parsnips, peeled and cut into 1½ x ¾-inch sticks

1 cup peeled, seeded, and diced (1-inch) butternut squash

2 medium zucchini, cut into 1½ x ¾-inch sticks

½ pound plum tomatoes (about 2 large), peeled, seeded, and cut into 1-inch dice

One 15-ounce can chickpeas, rinsed and drained

Kosher salt

1½ cups diced (½-inch) cooked turkey

¼ cup golden seedless raisins

½ cup lightly packed fresh cilantro leaves

1¾ cups water

2 tablespoons unsalted butter

½ pound (1¼ cups) couscous

Sambal oelek (Indonesian chile paste) or hot sauce, for serving

In a small, dry Dutch oven over medium heat, toast the saffron until fragrant, about 1 minute. Stir in the turmeric, cinnamon stick, chile, and stock; bring to a boil over high heat. Reduce the heat, cover, and simmer for 10 minutes. Add the onion, carrots, parsnips, and squash; continue simmering, covered, for 10 minutes. Add the zucchini and tomatoes, cover, and simmer until all the vegetables are just tender, about another 5 minutes (you may need to raise the heat to return the liquid to a simmer). When the vegetables are tender, stir in the chickpeas, ½ teaspoon salt, the turkey, raisins, and cilantro. Remove the pot from the heat and let sit, covered, until everything is heated through, about 5 minutes. Adjust the seasonings if needed.

Meanwhile, make the couscous. In a medium saucepan over high heat, bring the water to a boil, along with 1 teaspoon salt and 1 tablespoon of the butter. Stir in the couscous, cover tightly, remove from the heat, and let sit for 5 minutes. Cut the remaining 1 tablespoon butter into small pieces and scatter them over the couscous. Cover and let sit for 3 minutes. Fluff with a fork.

Mound a large spoonful of the couscous in a shallow soup bowl and ladle the turkey, vegetables, and stock over it. Serve with the sambal oelek on the side. —JENNIFER MCLAGAN

Shredded Turkey & Arugula Caesar Salad WITH GRILLED CROUTONS

SERVES 4

Here's a fresh take on Caesar salad that pairs mild turkey with spicy arugula. Only make this salad if you can find rich, green, unwilted arugula and tomatoes that have some sweet-tart personality; don't use insipid pale winter tomatoes. Many varieties of cherry tomato are surprisingly tasty during the winter season.

¼ pound baby arugula (about 5 cups loosely packed), washed and dried

2 tablespoons plus 2 teaspoons fresh lemon juice (from 1 large lemon)

2 teaspoons finely grated lemon zest

4 oil-packed anchovy fillets

2 large cloves garlic, crushed and peeled

¼ teaspoon black peppercorns

½ cup extra-virgin olive oil

1 tablespoon Dijon mustard

Kosher salt

½ cup finely grated Parmigiano-Reggiano

4 slices French baguette, cut 1 inch thick on an extreme diagonal (6 to 8 inches long)

2 cups shredded cooked turkey

2 cups halved cherry tomatoes

Heat a gas grill or the broiler. Put the arugula in a large bowl, cover with a damp paper towel, and refrigerate.

In a blender, combine the lemon juice and zest, anchovies, garlic, and peppercorns with 6 tablespoons of the oil, the mustard, and ½ teaspoon salt. Blend thoroughly until most of the peppercorns are well broken up and the dressing is emulsified. Add 2 tablespoons of the Parmigiano and blend to incorporate. Leave the dressing in the blender.

Brush the bread with the remaining 2 tablespoons oil and season with salt. Grill or broil the bread until dark around the edges and golden brown in the center, 1 to 2 minutes per side. Cut each bread slice into 10 cubes.

Pulse the dressing in the blender; add a little of it to the arugula, and toss to coat. Divide the arugula among four plates and sprinkle with a little of the Parmigiano. Toss the turkey and tomatoes with the remaining dressing and arrange over the arugula. Sprinkle with the remaining Parmigiano and arrange the croutons and tomatoes around the salad.

— ADAPTED FROM SUSIE MIDDLETON

Turkey & Blue Cheese Salad with TARRAGON-MUSTARD VINAIGRETTE

SERVES 4

This salad is delicious served with spears of Belgian endive, but tender leaves from romaine hearts work, too. You can also skip the greens altogether and serve some crispbread crackers or slices of whole-grain artisan bread.

FOR THE SALAD:

2 cups diced (½-inch) cooked turkey

1 cup thinly sliced celery hearts, including leaves

⅓ cup sliced almonds, toasted in a dry skillet over medium heat until lightly golden

1 sweet apple (such as Honeycrisp or Fuji), cored and cut into ½-inch dice

2 ounces creamy blue cheese (try Roquefort or Maytag Blue), crumbled (about ½ cup)

1 large Belgian endive, separated into spears

FOR THE VINAIGRETTE:

2 teaspoons finely chopped fresh tarragon

2 teaspoons grainy Dijon mustard

2 tablespoons tarragon vinegar

6 tablespoons olive oil

¼ teaspoon kosher salt; more to taste

Freshly ground black pepper

In a large bowl, toss the turkey, celery, almonds, and apple. Add the blue cheese.

Whisk the vinaigrette ingredients in a small bowl; taste and adjust the seasonings. Pour over the turkey mixture and toss well; taste and adjust the seasonings. Serve with the endive spears on the side.

—JENNIFER MCLAGAN

Turkey Cakes
WITH SPICY ROASTED TOMATO SALSA
SERVES 4

These tender-on-the-inside, crusty-on-the-outside cakes are great with a salad for lunch, or even tucked between two slices of bread or wrapped in a warm flour tortilla with some shredded lettuce. Or you could shape smaller patties and serve them with drinks.

1⅓ cups diced (½-inch) cooked turkey

2 tablespoons chopped fresh cilantro

1 tablespoon finely chopped fresh chives or finely diced scallion

1 fresh red or green chile (like a serrano or jalapeño), cored, seeded, and finely diced

1 cup fresh breadcrumbs

Grated zest of 1 lime

2 tablespoons fresh lime juice

3 tablespoons leftover turkey gravy (or heavy cream)

Kosher salt and freshly ground black pepper

1 large egg, separated

1 tablespoon cold water

¼ cup fine cornmeal

¼ cup olive oil

Spicy Roasted Tomato Salsa (page 221)

Put the diced turkey in a food processor and pulse until very finely chopped. Transfer to a medium bowl and add the cilantro, chives or scallion, chile, breadcrumbs, lime zest, lime juice, and gravy or cream; mix until well combined. Season with ¾ teaspoon salt and pepper to taste. Mix in the egg yolk. With wet hands, mold the mixture into eight patties ½ inch thick; they should only just hold together. Cover with plastic wrap and refrigerate for 30 minutes.

Put a baking sheet in the oven and heat the oven to 350°F. Put the cornmeal in a shallow bowl. Whisk the egg white with the water. Dip the patties into the egg white and then coat with the cornmeal.

Heat a large frying pan over medium heat; add the oil and, when it's hot, add the patties (work in batches if necessary). Cook on each side until golden, about 2 minutes per side. Transfer the patties to the heated baking sheet in the oven. Bake until heated through, about 5 minutes. Serve with the roasted tomato salsa. —JENNIFER MCLAGAN

=⚬⚬=

SPICY ROASTED TOMATO SALSA

For a milder sauce, remove the chile's ribs and seeds before chopping.

3 large plum tomatoes (about ¾ pound total), cored

1 fresh hot red or green chile (like serrano), ribs and seeds included, finely chopped

1 tablespoon chopped fresh cilantro

1 tablespoon fresh lime juice

½ teaspoon kosher salt

Freshly ground black pepper

YIELDS ABOUT 1 CUP

Heat the oven to 400°F. Cut the tomatoes in half lengthwise and remove the seeds. Set them cut side down on a foil-lined baking sheet and cook until the skins split and the tomatoes soften, about 10 minutes. Let them cool slightly before removing their skins. Put the skinned tomatoes in the food processor with the remaining ingredients. Process until well blended. Adjust the seasonings and serve alongside the turkey cakes.

Turkey Enchiladas WITH
CREAMY TOMATILLO SAUCE | SERVES 4

More and more grocery stores carry authentic Mexican cheeses, so look in the specialty dairy area for queso panela or queso añejo. Use one or a combination of the two instead of the mozzarella and provolone.

2 cups shredded cooked turkey (start with dark meat and add as much white meat as needed)

Kosher salt

Vegetable oil as needed

12 small (6-inch) corn tortillas

Creamy Tomatillo Sauce (page 223)

1 cup grated mozzarella

⅓ cup grated provolone

Season the shredded turkey with a little salt, if needed.

Fill a large skillet with enough oil to submerge a tortilla (between ¼ and ½ inch). Warm the oil over medium heat until a drop of water sizzles immediately. Fry each tortilla briefly in the oil, about 10 seconds per side. Use a metal spatula rather than tongs to flip the tortillas, as they'll tear easily. The tortilla should stay soft; if it starts to harden, it has been in the oil too long. Drain on paper towels.

Heat the oven to 400°F. With a pastry brush, spread a thin layer of sauce on both sides of each tortilla. Spoon a heaping 1 tablespoon of shredded turkey just off center of each tortilla and roll into loose cylinders. Set the enchiladas side by side in a 9x13-inch baking dish, pour the remaining sauce over them, top with the cheeses, and bake until bubbling and parts are lightly browned, 15 to 20 minutes. —ADAPTED FROM JIM PEYTON

=✂=

CREAMY TOMATILLO SAUCE

The addition of heavy cream or crème fraîche qualifies enchiladas made with this sauce as enchiladas suizas (Swiss-style enchiladas). The sauce can be made ahead and refrigerated for up to two days or frozen for up to a month.

1 pound fresh tomatillos, husks and stems removed, rinsed

2 or 3 fresh serrano chiles or 1 to 2 fresh jalapeños, cored and seeded

Four ¼-inch-thick slices white onion

3 cloves garlic, peeled

2 tablespoons chopped fresh cilantro

2 tablespoons vegetable oil

3 cups Roasted Turkey Stock (page 212) or homemade or low-salt chicken broth

¾ cup heavy cream or crème fraîche

¾ teaspoon kosher salt; more to taste

YIELDS ABOUT 3½ CUPS

Position a rack as close to the broiler as possible and heat the broiler. Arrange the tomatillos, chiles, onion slices, and garlic in a small, shallow baking pan. Broil, turning to ensure even cooking, until the tomatillos are soft and slightly blackened, about 10 minutes. Transfer the broiled ingredients to a blender and add the cilantro. Blend until smooth.

Heat the oil in a medium saucepan over medium-high heat. Add the tomatillo mixture and cook, stirring, for 2 to 3 minutes. Add 2 cups of the stock and simmer until the sauce is thick enough to coat the back of a spoon, about 20 minutes. Taste the sauce. It should be a little tart, but it shouldn't make your mouth pucker. If it's too tart, add more stock and simmer until the sauce thickens again. Remove from the heat and whisk in the heavy cream or crème fraîche and the salt. Let cool slightly before making the enchiladas.

ROASTED POBLANO & BELL PEPPER
Turkey Tacos

SERVES 2 AMPLY OR
4 AS A LIGHT MEAL

Feel free to play around with the toppings for this quick and casual dish: Sautéed corn would be a nice addition, while shredded beef or cooked diced potatoes could take the place of the turkey.

½ red bell pepper, cored, seeded, and flattened

1 poblano chile, cored, seeded, and flattened

2 tablespoons extra-virgin olive oil

½ teaspoon ground cumin

Pinch cayenne

1 clove garlic, put though a garlic press or minced

Juice of ½ lime

Pinch kosher salt

1½ cups shredded cooked turkey, mostly dark meat

½ cup sour cream

1 tablespoon finely chopped yellow onion

2 tablespoons finely chopped fresh cilantro; more for garnish

4 small (6- to 7-inch) corn tortillas

¼ cup grated Cheddar

Homemade or purchased tomato salsa for serving

Position an oven rack close to the broiler and heat the broiler. Put the bell pepper and the poblano skin side up on a baking sheet and broil until blackened. Transfer the peppers to a small bowl, cover with plastic wrap, and let cool. Reduce the oven temperature to 400°F.

In a medium bowl, combine the oil, cumin, cayenne, half of the garlic, and the lime juice. Season with salt. Add the turkey to the bowl and toss to coat it well with the vinaigrette.

When the peppers are cool enough to handle, remove the blackened skin and chop the peppers finely.

In a small bowl, combine the sour cream, onion, the remaining garlic, the cilantro, and chopped peppers.

Put the tortillas on a baking sheet. Divide the turkey mixture among the tortillas, leaving a little space around the edges. Top with the sour cream mixture, then the cheese. Bake until the cheese is melted, about 5 minutes. Garnish with a little fresh cilantro and serve with some salsa. Eat as is with a knife and fork or roll the tortilla up and eat with your hands. —ADAPTED FROM JOANNE SMART

Pasta Shells
WITH TURKEY, MUSHROOMS & CAPERS

SERVES 2
GENEROUSLY

This earthy, savory pasta dish is a great place to use good-quality salt-cured capers (soaked in water for 15 minutes and rinsed), if you can find them.

½ ounce dried porcini mushrooms, soaked in 1¼ cups warm water for 30 minutes

2 tablespoons olive oil

3 tablespoons unsalted butter

¼ pound fresh button mushrooms, wiped clean, stems trimmed, and sliced

1 large shallot, thinly sliced

1 clove garlic, minced

1½ teaspoons chopped fresh rosemary

Kosher salt and freshly ground black pepper

½ cup dry white wine

6 to 8 ounces dried pasta shells or farfalle

Splash of sherry vinegar

2 tablespoons capers, rinsed

1 cup diced (½-inch) cooked turkey

Grated Pecorino Romano, for serving (optional)

Strain the porcini, reserving the soaking liquid. Squeeze them dry, chop them into small pieces, and set aside. Strain the soaking liquid through a fine sieve or a coffee filter; set aside. Bring a large pot of salted water to a boil.

Meanwhile, in a large skillet over medium-high heat, heat the oil and 2 tablespoons of the butter. When the butter has melted, add the fresh mushrooms and cook, stirring frequently, until lightly browned and most of their liquid has evaporated, about 5 minutes. Add the shallot, garlic, rosemary, and chopped porcini. Cook, stirring, until the shallot is soft, about 4 minutes. Pour in the wine and the reserved porcini soaking liquid; bring to a boil and cook until the liquid is reduced by more than half. Taste; if it's not flavorful enough, continue reducing a bit more.

Meanwhile, cook the pasta until just tender. Drain the pasta and add it to the skillet. Add the vinegar, capers, and turkey, toss to coat everything, and heat gently for a few minutes. Stir in the remaining 1 tablespoon butter; taste again and adjust the vinegar, salt, and pepper. Serve warm with the grated Romano, if you like.

— ADAPTED FROM MOLLY STEVENS

Baked Rotini
WITH TURKEY, ASPARAGUS & SUN-DRIED TOMATOES

SERVES 6 TO 8

This hearty yet bright-tasting pasta dish is a delicious destination for leftover turkey. Because the turkey cooks for a few minutes in the sauce, dark meat is the best choice, because it won't dry out as much, but you can use a mix of white and dark if necessary.

2 to 3 tablespoons olive oil

2 cups diced (½-inch) cooked turkey, mostly dark meat

Kosher salt and freshly ground black pepper

1 to 2 cloves garlic, to your taste, minced

1½ cups Quick but Rich Turkey Giblet Broth (page 56) or homemade or low-salt chicken broth

1 cup heavy cream

2 tablespoons sherry vinegar

¼ cup drained and thinly sliced oil-packed sun-dried tomatoes

¼ cup coarsely chopped fresh basil

½ pound asparagus, cut into 1-inch pieces

1 pound dried rotini

2 cups grated Pecorino Romano

1½ cups grated mozzarella

½ cup coarse fresh breadcrumbs

Position a rack in the middle of the oven and heat the oven to 450°F. Grease a 9x13-inch baking dish with 1 tablespoon of the oil.

Heat 1 tablespoon of the oil in a 6- to 8-quart Dutch oven and sauté the turkey for just a minute to warm it through. Season it lightly with salt and pepper if needed. Using a metal spatula or a wooden spoon, push the turkey to the side. If the pan is dry, add another 1 tablespoon oil and then the garlic and cook until the garlic just starts to sizzle and becomes fragrant, about 10 seconds. Add the broth, cream, and 1 teaspoon salt. Bring to a boil over medium-high heat, reduce to a gentle simmer, and cook for 10 minutes, stirring occasionally, so that the sauce thickens slightly. Add the vinegar, sun-dried tomatoes, and basil and cook for about 5 minutes. Taste for salt and pepper, adding more if you like.

Meanwhile, bring a large pot of well-salted water to a boil. Add the asparagus and cook until just barely tender. Remove the asparagus with a slotted spoon and then cook the pasta in the same boiling water until it's just tender to the tooth, a little less than you normally might because it will cook more in the oven later.

Drain the pasta and add it to the sauce, along with the asparagus. Add half of the Pecorino and mozzarella to the pasta mixture and toss well. Transfer to the baking dish and spread evenly. Top the pasta with the remaining cheeses and the breadcrumbs. Bake until the cheese is golden brown and the breadcrumbs are golden brown and crisp, about 15 minutes. Let rest for 10 minutes before serving. —ADAPTED FROM TONY ROSENFELD

Contributors

Fine Cooking would like to thank all the talented and generous contributors who have shared their recipes with our readers.

Pam Anderson, a contributing editor for *Fine Cooking*, is also the author of many cookbooks, including *The Perfect Recipe*. She is the food columnist for *USA Weekend* magazine.

Jennifer Armentrout, a graduate of the Culinary Institute of America, is the editor of *Fine Cooking* magazine.

John Ash teaches wine training and cooking classes around the world. His latest book is *Cooking One on One: Private Lessons from a Master Teacher.*

Greg Atkinson is the former chef at Seattle's Canlis restaurant, a restaurant consultant, and the author of five cookbooks, including *West Coast Cooking.*

Ben & Karen Barker are chef-owners of the Magnolia Grill in Durham, North Carolina. They are the authors of *Not Afraid of Flavor.*

Paul Bertolli is the former chef of Chez Panisse restaurant in Berkeley and Oliveto in Oakland, California. He is the author of *Cooking by Hand* and the founder and curemaster of Fra' Mani Hand-Crafted Salumi.

Michael Brisson is the chef of l'Etoile restaurant in Martha's Vineyard.

Robert Carter is the chef of the Peninsula Grill in Charleston, South Carolina.

Regan Daley is a Toronto-based pastry chef and the author of the award-winning book *In the Sweet Kitchen.*

Tasha DeSerio was a cook at Chez Panisse for five years. She currently teaches, writes about cooking, and is the proprietor of Olive Green Catering in Berkeley.

Abigail Johnson Dodge is a contributing editor to *Fine Cooking* and author of *Desserts 4 Today* and *Mini Treats & Hand-Held Sweets*. Abby was the founding director of *Fine Cooking*'s test kitchen.

Beth Dooley is a food and garden writer based in Minneapolis; she is the co-author with chef Lucia Watson of *Savoring the Seasons of the Northern Heartland.*

Tom Douglas is the owner of five Seattle restaurants, including Dahlia Lounge, and the author of three cookbooks, including, most recently, *I Love Crab Cakes.*

Janet Fletcher trained at the Culinary Institute of America and cooked at Chez Panisse. She is a staff food writer for the *San Francisco Chronicle* and the author of 18 cookbooks.

Larry Forgione was one of the pioneers of the "new American cuisine," championing the use of high quality local ingredients and traditional American recipes. He is the chef/owner of An American Place in St. Louis, Missouri.

Gale Gand is a pastry chef, co-owner of Chicago's Tru restaurant, Food Network host, and cookbook author.

Laura Giannatempo is a former assistant editor at *Fine Cooking* and author of *A Ligurian Kitchen.*

Joyce Goldstein is a food writer, cookbook author, cooking teacher, and restaurant consultant. Her most recent book is *Antipasti.*

Susan Goss is the chef/owner of West Town Tavern in Chicago, Illinois.

Julianna Grimes is a freelance food writer and recipe developer and has a food consulting business, Flavor Matters, Inc.

Gordon Hamersley is the chef-owner of Hamersley's Bistro in Boston and author of the award-winning *Bistro Cooking at Home.*

Lisa Hanauer is a former chef-restaurateur living in Oakland, California.

Martha Holmberg is a cookbook author and recipe developer. She is the former editor and publisher of *Fine Cooking.*

Jill Silverman Hough is a food writer, recipe developer, and a cooking instructor at Copia: the American Center for Wine, Food and the Arts in Napa, California.

Arlene Jacobs is a chef and cooking teacher in New York City.

Sarah Jay is the former managing editor of *Fine Cooking.*

Wendy Kalen is a food stylist, recipe developer, and the senior editor for food at BHG.com, the website of *Better Homes and Gardens*.

Eva Katz has worked as a chef, caterer, teacher, recipe developer and tester, food stylist, and food writer. She is on the advisory board of the Cambridge School of Culinary Arts.

Elinor Klivans is a baking teacher and author of many cookbooks on desserts and pastries; her latest book is *Pot Pies: Yumminess in a Dish.*

Ris Lacoste is the award-winning executive chef of 1789 Restaurant in Washington, D.C. A member of the National Board of Directors for the American Institute of Wine and Food, Ris also serves on the board of the Marriott Hospitality Public Charter High School.

Seen Lippert is a former cook at Chez Panisse and chef at several New York restaurants. She's a member of Yale University's Sustainable Food Project.

Ruth Lively is a contributor to *Fine Cooking* and the former editor of *Fine Gardening* magazine.

Lori Longbotham is a food writer and the author of several cookbooks, including *Luscious Chocolate Desserts*.

Michael Louchen is the corporate chef for The Taunton Press.

Jeff Madura is the executive chef of John Ash Restaurant in Santa Rosa, California.

Jennifer McLagan is a Toronto-based food writer and stylist and author of the IACP award-winning cookbook *Bones*.

Alice Medrich is a leading authority on chocolate, the founder of the Berkeley, California, bakery Cocolat, a cookbook author, and cooking teacher.

Susie Middleton is a cookbook author, the former editor of *Fine Cooking*, and a blue-ribbon graduate of the Institute of Culinary Education (formerly Peter Kump's New York Cooking School).

Diane Morgan is a cooking teacher, restaurant consultant, and author of many cookbooks, including *The Thanksgiving Table*.

Orlando Murrin is the former editor of *BBC Good Food Magazine,* in London, England.

Micol Negrin is the former editor-in-chief *The Magazine of La Cucina Italiana*. She is a cooking teacher, cookbook author, and the founder of a culinary tour company.

Scott Peacock is the executive chef of Georgia's Watershed restaurant and co-author with Edna Lewis of *The Gift of Southern Cooking*.

Jim Peyton is a Mexican cooking authority, restaurant consultant, and cookbook author.

Scott Phillips graduated from Rochester Institute of Technology with a BFA in professional photographic illustration. He's the photography manager for The Taunton Press and an integral part of the *Fine Cooking* team.

Michelle Polzine is a San Francisco-based pastry chef.

Randall Price is a private chef with clients in Paris and Auvergne and the former chef to the American ambassador to Hungary.

Rebecca Rather, known as The Pastry Queen, is the owner of Rather Sweet Bakery in the Texas Hill Country town of Fredericksburg, and author of *The Pastry Queen*.

Nicole Rees co-wrote the revised edition of *Understanding Baking* and *The Baker's Manual*. She works as a food writer and food technologist in Portland, Oregon.

Leslie Revsin was the first woman chef at New York's Waldorf-Astoria hotel. She worked at other notable New York restaurants, then became a noted cookbook author and cooking teacher.

Tony Rosenfeld, a contributing editor to *Fine Cooking*, is a food writer and restaurant consultant in Boston. His latest cookbook is *Sear, Sauce & Serve*.

Maria Helm Sinskey is the former chef of San Francisco's PlumpJack Cafe and author of *In The Vineyard Kitchen*. She oversees the culinary programs at Napa Valley's Robert Sinskey Vineyards, which she owns with her husband.

Joanne McAllister Smart is special issues editor for *Fine Cooking* and co-author of *New Italian Cooking* and *Bistro Cooking at Home*.

Molly Stevens, a cooking teacher, cookbook author, and contributing editor to *Fine Cooking*, is the author of the award-winning *All About Braising*.

Kathleen Stewart is a member of The Baker's Dozen, a San Francisco Bay-area group of professional bakers and pastry experts; she's the owner of the acclaimed Downtown Bakery in Healdsburg, California.

Bill Telepan graduated from the Culinary Institute of America and was the executive chef at Manhattan's Judson Grill. He is now the chef/owner of Telepan, on Manhattan's Upper West Side.

Rori Trovato is a food stylist and author of *Dishing with Style*. She teaches cooking in Provence in summer and lives in Santa Barbara, California.

Carole Walter is a master baker, baking instructor, and award-winning cookbook author.

Lucia Watson is the chef-owner of Lucia's restaurant in Minneapolis. She frequently partners with writer Beth Dooley on projects, including their cookbook *Savoring the Seasons of the Northern Heartland*.

Carolyn Weil was the first pastry chef for Jeremiah Tower at the acclaimed Stars restaurant. She is a founding member of The Baker's Dozen, a San Francisco Bay-area group of professional bakers and pastry experts, and she teaches baking around the country.

Laura Werlin is a leading expert on American cheeses. She's the author of several cookbooks, including the award-winning *The New American Cheese*. Laura is on the board of the American Cheese Society.

Barbara Witt is a cookbook author whose books include *The Weekend Chef*. She is the co-author of *George Foreman's Big Book of Grilling, BBQ & Rotisserie*.

Index

Index

Index